EXPERIENCING FLOW

Life Beyond Boredom and Anxiety

by Susan A. Jackson, PhD

Permissions.

Table 1 adapted, by permission from Susan A. Jackson, "Factors influencing the occurrence of flow in elite athletes." *Journal of Applied Sport Psychology,* (1995): 138-166. Table adapted by permission from Informa UK Ltd, trading as Taylor & Francis Group.

Figure 1 adapted, by permission from S.A. Jackson and M. Csikszentmihalyi, *Flow in Sports* (Champaign, IL: Human Kinetics, 1999); and Csikszentmihalyi, M. and Csikszentmihalyi, I. Introduction to part IV. In *Optimal Experience: Psychological studies of flow in consciousness.* (New York: Cambridge University Press, 1988). Adapted with permission of the licensor through PLS Clear.

Figure 2 adapted, by permission from Massimini, F., and Carli, M. The systematic assessment of flow in daily experience. In Csikszentmihalyi, M. and Csikszentmihalyi, I. *Optimal experience: Psychological studies of flow in consciousness* (New York: Cambridge University Press, 1988). Adapted with permission of the licensor through PLS Clear.

Susan A. Jackson, author.
Title: Experiencing Flow: Life Beyond Boredom and Anxiety.
First published in 2024 by Authors on Mission, New York.
Visit the author's websites at www.drsuejackson.com and www.bodyandmindflow.com.au

Copyright © Susan A. Jackson 2024

First Edition

ISBNs:
978-1-950336-84-5 - Kindle
978-1-950336-82-1 - Paperback
978-1-950336-83-8 - Hardback

All rights reserved. No part of this publication may be reproduced, stored in a retrieval system, or transmitted, in any form or by any means, without the prior written permission of the publisher.

Published by Authors on Mission

"*Experiencing Flow* is a powerful catalyst for embracing the concept and application of flow in our daily lives. Seamlessly weaving together insightful research, poignant personal anecdotes, and a spirit of exploration, Sue eloquently underscores the fundamental truth that the essence of a fulfilling life lies in the richness of our moment-to-moment experiences. In an age defined by the incessant tug of distractions and the pervasive grip of anxiety, Sue's timely insights call us to reassess our connection with the present moment, guiding us toward a journey of deeper fulfillment and heightened purpose."

—*Hazel Findlay, Professional Climber, Coach, & Founder of Strong Mind*

"For those familiar with the concept of flow, you'll find this book a wonderful review of all that makes up the flow experience. For those unfamiliar with "flow," this book reveals the full meaning of flow as a part of the human experience. With engaging and accessible prose, Sue Jackson takes the reader on a refreshing and insightful journey about flow, that space between anxiety and boredom, presented with clarity and accessibility. Sue explains in vivid terms how, in a world filled with stress and distractions, you can learn to experience flow through mindfulness to bring you peace and happiness. That's worth discovering."

—*Rainer Martens, Founder, Human Kinetics Publishers*

"Sue Jackson offers an essential contribution to the understanding of flow, debunking several myths and misconceptions, and highlighting its role as a key psychological construct. She achieves this goal through an engaging narrative, as well as a rigorous writing style, appealing to researchers, practitioners, and any reader interested in the topic. A comprehensive view of flow is provided, which takes shape throughout the chapters through the words of Mihaly Csikszentmihalyi, who shed brilliant light on this pervasively optimal experience; and also through the words of people encountered by Sue in her research and practice of sport psychology, mindfulness, and psychotherapy."

—*Antonella Delle Fave, M.D., Professor of Psychology, Faculty of Medicine, University of Milan*

"Flow is a fascinating and important construct for human well-being. Sue Jackson is a world expert on flow and has written an accessible book not only explaining flow itself (including what it is not) but relating it to other important issues, including acceptance, goals, mindfulness, and growth mindset. Things are brought to life with some great quotes and references to interesting life experiences. It's a great read. You will learn a lot – I did!"

—*Stuart J.H. Biddle, Professor of Physical Activity & Health, University of Southern Queensland*

"As a passionate flow practitioner, this is the book I have been waiting for. Dr. Sue Jackson is one of the world's leading authorities on flow having worked with and learnt from the best—the father of flow—Mihaly Csikszentmihalyi. Her book not only honours his legacy, but it sets the record straight on what flow is and is not and addresses the current trend of sensationalizing the experience reminding us that flow state cannot be simply switched on or forced. The book is packed with research examples and quotes, including her own research and that of other leading scientists, from this important area of psychology. Her more recent interviews with leading experts and athletes add to the richness of this text and brings flow right up to date. If you want to live a better and more fulfilling life, then this book is an essential read. And just like the many great works of Csikszentmihalyi himself, it is a book to be referred to again and again."

—*Derek Tate, MSc, President Professional Ski Instructors of Europe (PSIE)*

"*Experiencing Flow* is a wonderful book and will contribute to a better understanding of the flow experience. Sue has detailed key areas that impact flow and the many real-life examples clearly illustrate the principles for finding flow—and the quotes are enriching in every sense. Importantly, Sue has honoured the work of Csikszentmihalyi beautifully. This book captures the essentials all should gather to understand flow better. Mihaly Csikszentmihalyi gave the world a gift and psychology a direction. Sue's book adds to Mihaly's timeless contribution."

—*John Hendry, OAM, Former Director of Student Welfare, Geelong Grammar School*

"Expert advice on flow that takes us "beyond boredom and anxiety" is as important today as it was when Mihaly Csikszentmihalyi first wrote about flow in the 1970s. Dr. Sue Jackson's book, *Experiencing Flow: Life Beyond Boredom and Anxiety*, provides the most up-to-date guidance available for flow seekers. Through an expert synthesis of research, case studies, psychological practice, and personal experience, Dr. Jackson shows that flow is accessible to all of us through the course of life—including during times of adversity. This important volume illuminates the key ingredients of flow, provides very practical strategies toward attaining flow, and offers many opportunities for self-reflection and planning to authentically map key lessons learned into everyday life."

—*Andrew J. Martin, PhD, Professor of Educational Psychology, University of New South Wales*

"*Experiencing Flow* is a must-read for psychology practitioners and researchers, as well as individuals interested in living a more fulfilling life. Performance psychologist Sue Jackson, who has studied flow for four decades, combines her knowledge of the topic with her own personal experiences and interviews she conducted with elite performers and other researchers in the field. The book begins with a tribute to Mihaly Csikszentmihalyi, who introduced the world to flow. In doing so, it provides a glimpse of how a great scientist thinks, capturing his experience and thinking that led to the idea of flow and flow theory. Mindfulness as a vehicle for achieving flow is also discussed in detail, with Jackson providing very practical guidelines for doing so. The book finishes by discussing how flow can help all of us live a more fulfilling life in the hectic information age in which we live. Reading the book will certainly help all of us do so."

—*Daniel Gould, Gwen Norrell Professor Emeritus of Youth Sport & Student Athlete Wellness, Michigan State University*

"Sue Jackson leaves no doubt how special flow experience is, while expertly making the case that flow—optimal experience—is not just for "special" people. Sue shares incredibly rich stories and strategies so that we can learn what elite performers know about tapping into our best selves to rise to new challenges, the ones we take on eagerly and the ones that take us by surprise. From how we think about ourselves, to how we pay attention in each moment, to how we breathe, this book teaches that we have many resources we can use to become better than we are right now—while transforming anxiety and boredom into presence, meaning, and joy."

—*Deanne Gute, PhD, Co-founder, The Flow Channel Foundation & TheFlowChannel.com*

"Dr. Jackson takes the academic concept of flow and applies it to anyone interested in improving the quality of their life. She shows how the popular concept of mindfulness gets you ready to enter a flow state and provides practical mindfulness strategies for experiencing flow. She demonstrates that to experience flow is to experience complete absorption in the task at hand, where skills and abilities are matched with task difficulty, and one performs effortlessly. With lots of informative quotes from performers in different domains, entertaining anecdotes, and what we know from research, Dr. Jackson presents a comprehensive understanding of flow and how it can enhance our lives. It is a fun and informative read."

—*Bob Weinberg, Professor Emeritus, Miami University*

"My awareness of the depth of Dr. Sue Jackson's understanding of flow as a construct caused me to read *Experiencing Flow* with great anticipation and high expectations. I was not disappointed in the slightest. Dr. Jackson is a scientist-practitioner who has spent her career centering her research and professional practice on the elusive but highly valued experiential state that Mihaly Csikszentmihalyi labeled "flow". Perhaps unsurprisingly given the extent of her interactions and collaboration with Dr. Csikszentmihalyi, her depiction of his carefully considered conceptualization and theorizing on the flow state strikes me as thoroughly authentic and accurate. It is a depiction that is entirely accessible, at least in part, because Dr. Jackson included many relatable personal insights and disclosures from exceptionally skilled performers and practitioners intent on facilitating optimal experience among others. I particularly appreciated her intentionality in not only linking this sought after experiential state to optimal functioning, as most commonly occurs, but also to individual well-being, happiness, and ultimately the sense that one is experiencing a life that is meaningful and being well-lived. I recommend it strongly."

—*Robert C. Eklund, Mode L. Stone Distinguished Professor of Sport Psychology, Florida State University*

"In 1990 Mihaly Csikszentmihalyi gifted the world with his book *Flow*. In 2024, Sue Jackson offers us a second gift in *Experiencing Flow: Life Beyond Boredom and Anxiety*. In the intervening 34 years, science has taught us much about flow. Here, Sue takes us to a new place, weaving much of that knowledge with her own passion and experience. She shares clear and practical strategies for integrating flow with growth mindset and mastery perspective, mindfulness, meditation, breathwork, and Acceptance Commitment Therapy. The future of flow—and the good it can do for our world—will come from our ability to integrate flow with these practices. Learn how in Sue Jackson's important and necessary book!"

—*Gary Gute, PhD, Co-founder, The Flow Channel Foundation & TheFlowChannel.com; Professor of Human Development, University of Northern Iowa*

EXPERIENCING FLOW

Life Beyond Boredom and Anxiety

Dedication

To Jack and Sean, who have taught me that flow can be found in good times and bad.

Table of Contents

Preface 1

Chapter 1: Meeting "Mike" 4
    Life Beyond Boredom and Anxiety 4
    Remembering a Flow Experience 6
    Meeting Mike 9
    Diving Deep into Flow Research 9
    Summary of Factors Found to Influence Flow 12
    Why Quality of Experience Matters 15
    Writing *Flow in Sports* 16
    Work and Flow 18

Chapter 2: Remembering Mike and What He Taught Us About Flow 21
    Early Influences 21
    Bypassing Boredom and Anxiety at a Young Age 23
    Mike Brings the Flow Framework to the World 24
    The Impact of Mike's Work Described by People Who Knew Him Well 25
    Understanding Flow by Understanding the Father of Flow 28
    Lived Complexity 31
    A Life Well Lived 33

Chapter 3: So, What Is Flow and How Do You Know It Is Flow? .. 36
    Understanding Flow 36
    The Nine Dimensions of Flow 38
    Flow as Enjoyment 46

Recognizing Flow 48

Chapter 4: Understanding Flow Experience Through
the Challenge-Skill Balance Model 52

Models to Understand How Flow Occurs 53
Making the Model Practical 58
Self-assessment of Subjective Experience 59
It's Perceptions of Challenges and Skills That Matter 61
Go a Little Bit Out of Your Depth 62
Balancing Challenges and Skills: Self-Reflection Exercise 66

Chapter 5: Moving From Anxiety to Flow via Acceptance 68

Anxiety Gets to Most of Us at Least Some of the Time 68
Learning a Different Way to Relate to Anxiety through ACT 71
Live it to Learn It 73
Becoming Psychologically Flexible 78

Chapter 6: Moving From Boredom to Mastery and Flow 80

A Pathway Out of Boredom 80
Growth and Fixed Mindset 82
Understanding a Mastery Perspective through Task and Ego
Orientations 85
The Problem with Chronic Boredom 89

Chapter 7: Finding a Pathway to Flow via Mindfulness 91

Learning About Mindfulness 92
Mindfulness, Self-Awareness, and Flow 95
Mindfulness as an Essential Skill for the 21st Century 97
How Mindfulness Facilitates Flow: Scientific Evidence 100

Chapter 8: Practical Mindfulness Strategies for Finding Flow 105

Learning to Meditate 106
Breathing Awareness 108
The long exhale 110
The 4-part breath 110
Lengthening the breathing practice 111
Alternate nostril breathing 112
Body Awareness 113
Body scans 113
Yoga nidra 114
Letting Go of Thoughts 115
Integrative Meditative Practices 116
Mantra Music as a Pathway to Flow 117

Chapter 9: How Two Mindfulness Whisperers Helped Unlock Flow on the Basketball Court 120

Phil Jackson Brings Awareness of Flow to the NBA 120
Performance Whisperer George Mumford 122

Chapter 10: Flow in the Information Age 131

Flow Becomes Somewhat Mainstream 131
Access to Descriptions of Flow in the Information Age 133
What Flow is Not 139
Why Flow Makes Life Worth Living 140

Chapter 11: Experience Matters 145

Life is a Chain of Subjective Experiences 145
Learning to be Autotelic 147
What About the Experience of Adversity? 148

Take 2—A Personal Reminder of the Importance of Finding Meaning in Adversity 151
Christmas in hospital 152
Unwanted Challenges 153
The power of feedback 156
Learnings 157
Learning to Live with the Uncontrollables 160
Embracing Experience to Grow 161

Notes 164

Acknowledgments 175

Preface

To experience complete absorption in what you are doing, where nothing else seems to matter but the task in front of you, and to find that task unfolding effortlessly before you is to experience flow. Flow exists at the intersection of a personally challenging situation and a higher-than-usual level of skill, which you draw upon to meet the challenge. This combination of high challenge and high skill sets the flow experience apart from other experiences we encounter as we go through life. One such experience is boredom, defined through the flow model as occurring when our skills outweigh the challenge to such an extent that we lose focus and motivation. At the other extreme is the perhaps all-too-familiar experience of anxiety, where the challenge is perceived to be beyond our skills. Flow lies between these experiences of boredom and anxiety, and it brings to our lives a richness that elevates ordinary experiences to optimal.

I've written *Experiencing Flow: Life Beyond Boredom and Anxiety* to share what I have learned about flow through my many years of having worked with this optimal state, first as a researcher and later as a practicing performance psychologist. This book is for anyone interested in understanding flow through the lens of how it has been defined and described by the founder of flow, Mihaly Csikszentmihalyi. I was fortunate to know "Mike" Csikszentmihalyi as my mentor – and as the greatest thinker I've had the good fortune to spend time with. Twenty-five years ago, Mike and I co-authored *Flow in Sports: The Keys to Optimal Experiences and Performances*. Each of us had our first experiences with flow in the sport domain. In *Flow in Sports*, we combined our shared love of sport with our respective research on flow in athletes and within the world of sport.

Experiencing Flow is written for a wider audience than *Flow in Sports*. It is written for anyone wishing to expand their psychological potential through exploring that space where time and effort cease to exist. Where self-consciousness is lost, and enjoyment is most profound. Where focus is complete, and fear completely absent.

Individuals seeking optimal performance in any domain, be it sport, the arts, work, or everyday life, can find within these pages the ingredients for success. A success that is not only defined by the superior performance outcomes flow is associated with. Rather, a marker of success that goes beyond achievement to focus on the quality of experience encountered along the way. Flow is important for the quality of focused attention it provides when we reach beyond our usual benchmarks of what we perceive we can do in the face of high challenge. Flow allows us to build important skills and stretch our previously held limits.

The book begins with a historical account of how I came to understand flow and develop a passion for exploring the flow concept as a researcher. I begin with an overview of my first encounters with flow, and with the founder of flow, who was to become my mentor, Mihaly Csikszentmihalyi. I then share insights from some of the people who knew "Mike" Csikszentmihalyi best. A big motivation for writing this book was to honor Mike's tremendous work in bringing to the world the flow concept and to help advance his conceptualization of flow in a world where flow may either not be well understood, or accurately represented. I describe Mike's flow framework by overviewing the dimensions of flow and the all-important challenge-skill balance equation that operationally defines a flow experience.

In the middle of the book, I cover the experiences that can occur when our challenge-skill balance is not optimal: anxiety when our perceived challenges are too high and boredom when our skills outweigh the presenting challenges. Drawing on the psychological frameworks of Acceptance and Commitment Therapy (ACT) and achievement motivation research, I offer strategies to help one move out of anxiety or boredom and towards flow. Another psychological approach that I have found to be particularly helpful when the goal is to facilitate flow in our lives is mindfulness, and three chapters are devoted to the interplay between mindfulness and flow and how to make flow more likely through developing a mindfulness practice.

In the final sections of the book, I share some examples of how flow is becoming more widely referenced in many different sectors of life. I conclude the book by arguing why quality of experience matters as we go through our lives. And how, even in times of adversity, we can reclaim aspects of our experience that we have some control over, direct our attention toward finding our challenge-skill balance, and forge meaning in what life presents us with.

By understanding flow principles and practices that facilitate this optimal psychological state, we can create a life full of purpose and fulfillment. I hope you find in the reading of this book your own ways to live a flow-enriched life.

CHAPTER 1

Meeting "Mike"

Life Beyond Boredom and Anxiety

What is life like beyond the opposing experiences of boredom and anxiety? At the edges of either being bored or being anxious lies the potential for experiencing an optimal psychological state called flow. This book shares the wisdom about flow I've gained through my experiences from the time I first started to research it in the mid-1980s, to then writing a book on flow in sports with the founder of flow, to helping clients find flow in my work today as a performance psychologist.

I stumbled across the concept of flow by fortuitously finding a copy of the book *Beyond Boredom and Anxiety* on a library bookshelf. In the opening pages of *Beyond Boredom and Anxiety*, author Mihaly Csikszentmihalyi set out his purpose in this, his first book on flow:

> *The simple goal of this study is to understand enjoyment, here and now—not as compensation for past desires, not as preparation for future needs, but as an ongoing process which provides rewarding experiences in the present.*[1]

Reading *Beyond Boredom and Anxiety* opened the door to an experience I had long treasured but, prior to reading, did not have a language to describe or understand. In this first of his many insightful books, Csikszentmihalyi described for the first time an optimal subjective experience to which he gave the name "flow."

If you hesitated on the name of the author of *Beyond Boredom and Anxiety*, you are not alone. When presenting on flow and describing the

Meeting "Mike"

work of Mihaly Csikszentmihalyi, a reliable question from the audience was, "How do you pronounce that name?" Turns out, it is quite phonetic, "Chick-sent-me-high." However, throughout this book, I will interchangeably refer to Mihaly Csikszentmihalyi by this, his Hungarian name and the name he invited people in the West to call him: Mike. The fact that Csikszentmihalyi invited the West to use the name *Mike* demonstrates his desire to make himself and his work accessible, as do his many books on flow written for all readers interested in understanding this psychological state.

At the time of reading *Beyond Boredom and Anxiety*, I had not heard of flow—something I would go on to notice in most people with whom I shared the topic I was researching for my PhD in sport psychology. It has only been in more recent years that flow has been referred to in popular media as a state that most readers are anticipated to recognize.

I remember what I was doing while reading *Beyond Boredom and Anxiety* in early 1987. I had stumbled across the eye-catching title while perusing the bookshelves of the University of Illinois library. I was in the process of working out what my master's in psychology thesis was going to focus on, and I was in the library to collect a book on achievement motivation. On the shelf next to the book I was there to check out, I noticed an eye-catching title, and curious as to *what* was beyond boredom and anxiety, I borrowed the book and took it on a plane trip with me from Chicago to my hometown of Sydney, Australia. It was a long trip, and as I sometimes did in the 80s when flying (if I was lucky enough to score two empty seats next to me), I lay on the floor in front of my seat, engrossed in this book with a catchy title. I've never liked sitting, and when there was an option not to, even if it meant lying on the floor of a plane, I'd take it. Of course, it was a time of fewer restrictions than we face today when flying internationally, where someone lying on the floor is promptly told by flight attendants to get back in their seat!

Rather than finding the long flight home the seemingly endless experience it usually was, I became engrossed in a book that gave me a language for the most memorable moments in my life. Moments when I was so totally focused on what I was doing that there was nothing else taking up space in my usually over-active mind. Experiences where I felt strong, in control, and like I could do no wrong.

Remembering a Flow Experience

One of the more vivid of these flow experiences for me was competing in a 200m sprint final at the last State All-Schools Championships of my high school athletics career. I'd taken part in this competition every year throughout high school, and this was to be my final event. I went into the race determined to win and confident about doing so. But, from the moment the gun went off to when I crossed the tape first, it was only the process of the challenge that captured my complete focus. More than forty years on and I can still replay that race in my head in its entirety. From reacting quickly to the starter's gun to rounding the bend ahead of all the other competitors—and this was from the inside lane 1—to entering the straight and seeing nothing other than my lane and the white tape in the distance. The feeling of running fast effortlessly captured my entire sensory field, and as I crossed the tape, I felt a rush of excitement and joy, having experienced a perfect race. My school was positioned in the stands directly at the end of the track in line with the finish line, and I didn't slow down until I neared the fence. My own happiness was engulfed by the cheers of my school, and I high-fived dangling arms from above me and smiled with contentment. I had done it.

I had prepared well for that race, the final competition of my high school career. My confidence and my motivation were both high. Yet I had prepared well for other races, too. It was the mindset I brought to this race that was different. There were no self-doubts, only an intent focus on my goal and on what unfolded before me, seemingly without effort on my part.

> ### Recalling a Flow Experience
>
> *Self-reflection Exercise:* Can you recall a time when you felt totally absorbed in what you were doing, where you felt strong and confident, and looking back on your experience, remember it as a time of great enjoyment? Can you replay what you were doing in your mind's eye and recall the feeling of your performance?

Years later, I would remember that race, the details, and the almost magical feel to it. Then, in *Beyond Boredom and Anxiety*, I read of chess players so immersed in what they were doing that time disappeared. I felt like the normal passing of time was on pause during my race. One chess player in *Beyond Boredom and Anxiety* described how an adjoining internal wall fell down during his match, and he only realized it after he finished playing! During my race, I could hear nothing other than the sounds of running. I saw only the track in front of me and the competitors I passed. It was only on completing the race that I could hear the shouting and clapping of the spectators lining the stadium.

In *Beyond Boredom and Anxiety*, I read of mountain climbers feeling at one with the rock they ascended, dancers part of the music they moved to, and surgeons describing their work as enjoyable and absorbing, demonstrating that flow is not just reserved for sport or leisure activities. The similarity between the experiences of rock climbers, dancers, chess players, and surgeons was remarkable.

It was in this first book on flow that Mike provided an explanation for how people taking part in different activities could experience flow, and this explanation also shed light on the title of his book. Flow is encountered beyond the states of boredom or anxiety when challenges and skills are closely matched. When challenges exceed perceived capabilities, anxiety is experienced. And conversely, when skills are greater than the opportunities available to demonstrate them, boredom results. It was a simple but profound model.

After reading *Beyond Boredom and Anxiety*, I now had a name for this experience of total absorption in a task: Flow. I finished the book on my flight, and I now knew where my research focus was going to head—to understand this experience of flow in sport. For my master's research, I had already decided that I was going to be examining achievement motivation in Division I college athletes. Following reading *Beyond Boredom and Anxiety*, I added in the study of flow to my research on athletes' motivation and experience. I came up with a questionnaire that I hoped would tap into the athletes' flow experiences, and I decided to add a qualitative component to my research project by interviewing a sub-set of my sample about their flow experiences. Just as Mike had done in his ground-breaking first book on flow.

It was in these interviews for my master's research project that I realized flow was not just a special experience for me. All the athletes I interviewed spoke with passion about times they were in flow. And several, as we ended the interview, thanked me, the researcher, for asking them about what their experience in their sport was like. They'd comment that everyone was always interested in their results or some performance outcome. But rarely did they get asked about their experience while taking part in their chosen activity. The athletes' gratitude was marked, and it was a turning point for me as a researcher. I decided to conduct an in-depth qualitative investigation on flow for my PhD. At the time, qualitative research was not mainstream in sport psychology. I was fortunate to have in Professor Dan Gould a PhD advisor who himself saw the value in qualitative research and who encouraged me to pursue my particular research interests in my doctoral thesis. I was intrigued by the rich descriptions of being in flow I had obtained from athletes I interviewed in my first graduate degree and the clear value they placed on flow experience in their lives. I knew this was a topic I wanted to research further.

Meeting Mike

While reading *Beyond Boredom and Anxiety*, I noticed that the author, Csikszentmihalyi, was based in Chicago, a 3-hour drive from where I was studying for my master's degree at the University of Illinois at Urbana-Champaign (U of I). I decided to attempt to make contact with Mike, and in 1987, letters and phone calls were the primary forms of communication between people. Thus, I wrote a letter to Mike via the Psychology Department at the University of Chicago. To my surprise, I received a letter of reply soon after, with Mike encouraging me to pursue my idea of researching flow in sport. Mike invited me to telephone him to discuss this further, and so I apprehensively called the number he provided. I was greeted with a strong Hungarian accent, and an eminent professor welcoming my questions on flow. I was so happy to have had an opportunity to speak to Mike, and thus began my journey of learning about flow from the master himself.

My master's research demonstrated links between flow and perceptions of ability, as well as an orientation to personal mastery. Athletes who had high perceptions of ability and were motivated by personal goals and improvement were more likely to experience flow than athletes with lowered perceived ability and a focus on outperforming others. I shared my findings with Mike, and he was both interested in and encouraging of my research.

With my master's degree completed, my two main take-aways were that athletes were genuinely passionate about flow and that Mike was genuinely interested in my research endeavors. I had enjoyed my graduate studies and wanted to pursue further research on flow in sport via a PhD.

Diving Deep into Flow Research

After completing my Masters, I returned to my hometown of Sydney. I missed Australia and yet wanted to continue my post-grad studies.

After exploring options within Australia, I decided to return to the US to study with one of my professors from U of I, Dan Gould. Dan had moved from the U of I to the University of North Carolina—Greensboro (UNCG) and hence I got to experience the Southeast in the US. A very different life experience from the Midwest in Illinois.

Working with Dan as a research assistant on projects he was conducting with USA Wrestling, US Figure Skating, and the US Ski team, I experienced first-hand the richness that qualitative research data provided. I spent many hours sitting in Dan's office chair after Dan had left for the day, interviewing US national champion figure skaters about life at the top of their sport. This was a project Dan had developed after working with many national champion figure skaters and finding a consistent theme of high stress and difficulty coping upon reaching national champion status. I was Dan's main research assistant on this project, and at the time, I was concurrently developing my PhD thesis proposal on flow experience in elite athletes. Dan kindly allowed me to interview the skaters about their experience of flow at the end of the main interview.

Beautiful depictions of flow on ice, both as individuals and as pair/dance skaters, came from talking with these top-level performers about flow. For example, here's how a few of the skaters described their experience in flow:

> *It was actually very real . . . I knew every single moment; in fact, I even remember going down into a jump and this is awful, but thinking, "Oh gosh, this is so real! I'm so clear in my thoughts." There was just a real clarity to it all . . . I felt in such control of everything, of every little movement, I was very aware, you know, like what was on my hand, I could feel my rings, I could feel everything, and I felt I had control of anything.*

Meeting "Mike"

A pairs skater described experiencing flow with his partner:

The focus was so narrow because my partner was in the same focus, and it was just she and I skating... Everything else goes away; it almost happens in slow motion—even though you're doing things at the correct time with the music and everything. Nothing else matters, it's just such an eerie, eerie feeling.

Another skater described how, when in flow, there's the sense that nothing can go wrong:

Well, it's like practice you can sharpen it, make the razor thinner, but you can fall one way or the other — and I think that's like the stressors, they can tip it. But once you're in that groove, it just seems like nothing can go wrong you know.

- USA National Champion and Olympic Figure Skaters[2]

These elite figure skaters I interviewed clearly knew the experience of flow. Having learned so much about the importance of flow from interviewing athletes at the top of their sport, I decided to conduct a more extensive investigation of flow across seven sports for my doctoral research. The athletes I interviewed came from the sports of track and field, swimming, cycling, rugby union, field hockey, triathlon, and rowing. My interview consisted of four parts: the athletes' experience of flow, their perceived antecedents of flow, perceived disruptors of flow, and their thoughts on how their flow experiences, peak performances, and peak experiences were similar to and different from each other. The project generated mountains of interview transcripts, hours of synthesizing the interview data into over-arching themes, application of qualitative principles for establishing credibility and trustworthiness in the data, and finally, the big write-up.

The athletes' open-ended descriptions of flow fit nicely with Csikszentmihalyi's nine-dimensional flow model, lending support to the established flow literature base and demonstrating that the qualities of flow were experienced similarly across many different domains. This finding echoed what Mike detailed in *Beyond Boredom and Anxiety*—consistency in reported experience of flow. While playing basketball involves different demands from performing a surgical operation, in *Beyond Boredom and Anxiety,* the commonality in descriptions of being totally involved in one's activity of choice came through resoundingly. This was echoed in my PhD data with athletes across seven sports. Through an extensive inductive analysis of my interview data, I found strong support for the way in which Mike had described the flow experience as being made up of several consistent dimensions. These dimensions are detailed in Chapter 3.

Summary of Factors Found to Influence Flow

After asking athletes to describe what being in flow was like, I asked them to share the main factors influencing whether or not they experienced flow. Table 1 provides a summary of my PhD findings about the antecedents and disruptors of flow. Once someone is introduced to the concept of flow, they almost invariably want to experience more flow in their activity. This Table provides a summary of the overarching areas the elite athletes reported either help, prevent, or disrupt their flow experiences. These overarching areas were called general dimensions and were synthesized from a large amount of interview data from the athletes.

I summarized the factors athletes reported influenced whether or not flow occurred into these ten general dimensions:

1. Being highly motivated to perform
2. Achieving optimal arousal level before performing
3. Being well prepared, including having pre-competition plans and event-focus plans

4. Optimal physical preparation, readiness, and mental state
5. Optimal environmental and situational conditions and influences
6. Feeling positive during the performance
7. Being focused
8. Being confident and having a positive mental attitude
9. The team playing well and interacting with each other positively (for team sports/events)
10. Having experienced flow before (so I know what it is)

Factors that Help Flow	Factors that Prevent Flow	Factors that Disrupt Flow
Motivation to perform	Lacking motivation to perform	
Achieving optimal arousal level before competing	Non-optimal arousal level	
Pre-competitive/competitive plans and preparation	Problems with pre-competitive preparation	
Optimal physical preparation and readiness	Non-optimal physical preparation and readiness	Problems with physical readiness or physical state
Optimal environmental and situational conditions	Non-optimal environmental and situational conditions	Non-optimal environmental and situational influences
Performance feeling good	Performance going poorly	Performance errors/problems
Focus	Inappropriate focus	Inappropriate focus
Confidence and positive attitude	Lacking confidence and negative attitude	Doubting or putting pressure on self
Positive team play and interactions	Negative team play and interactions	Problems with team performance or interactions
Experience factor		

Table 1. *Factors Influencing Flow in Elite Athletes.* Adapted, with permission, from Jackson, 1995[3]

While this set of ten factors describes the factors influencing flow identified in my analysis of elite athlete interviews, most of the ten factors are relevant to domains outside of sport. Motivation and its corollary in high-performance situations, arousal level, impact what everyone does in an achievement setting. Being well prepared for an upcoming event, including planning out what you will be doing from both a physical and a psychological perspective, is another factor that crosses performance domains. The next factor, having optimal preparation and this leading to a positive mental state, is relevant across settings. The 5th factor, optimal environmental and situational conditions, is relevant to performers whose environment (including the social environment) influences their performance. The factors of feeling positive, being focused, and maintaining confidence, again, are relevant regardless of the performance arena. The team factor of how well the team is playing and interacting is, of course, only relevant where one's performance is situated within the performance of others. And finally, the flow experience factor—having experienced flow before so you know what the state is when it appears—is relevant, and this factor ties back to the focus on the present dimension. If one recognizes flow and starts saying to oneself, "Great, I am in flow!" the state will undoubtedly be lost.

My experience interviewing elite athletes provided me with rich data and led to several publications that I hope helped advanced understanding of flow. I found the experience of interviewing the athletes for my research studies among the most rewarding of my research career. My eyes were opened to what Mike had shared about what matters most about flow—the experience itself.

Why Quality of Experience Matters

"Optimal experience is the bottom line of existence."[4]

—*Csikszentmihalyi*

Note that Mike didn't write that optimal performance is what matters most, but rather optimal *experience*. It was the elite athletes I interviewed for my master's and then subsequently in my PhD research who demonstrated this to me. I had thought that for athletes at the top end of their sport, it would be their optimal performances that stood out for them, and certainly, such performances were important. However, a performance in flow was valued more highly than one not in flow.

And, as mentioned, for athletes at the end of being interviewed to stop and thank me for asking them about the quality of their experiences confirmed just how much experience mattered to them. The athletes I interviewed sincerely expressed gratitude for an opportunity to talk in-depth about those special moments when they were in flow. This insight struck me and helped me to recognize just how important quality of experience is. Csikszentmihalyi had written about this back in 1982:

> *It is useful to remember occasionally that life unfolds as a chain of subjective experiences . . . The quality of these experiences determines whether and to what extent life was worth living.*[5]

Flow is often associated with peak performance or performing at one's best. However, on interviewing athletes for my PhD on how they perceived the relationship between flow and peak performance, it became clear that while flow often led to a peak performance, it was also possible to have a strong performance without the experience of flow. For the athletes, this involved pushing hard, being lucky, or even gritting it out. The quality of such experiences was nowhere near as positive as when flow was present.

Sometimes, flow is also associated with a peak experience, a concept described by the ground-breaking psychology of experience researcher Abraham Maslow. Maslow defined peak experience as a moment of highest happiness. When I asked the athletes in my research their thoughts on how flow and peak experience related to each other, they saw that the two experiences often went together. In particular, the most memorable flow experiences athletes recalled were generally also regarded as being some of their happiest moments. However, the athletes mentioned that flow could occur without it being a peak experience, just as a peak experience might not be a flow experience. For example, a peak experience might occur from an athlete achieving something new or remarkable, which could be with or without flow present.

My PhD thesis was well-received within my field of sport psychology, and I enjoyed sharing my findings at conferences, and in research and applied publications. I was the recipient of two North American doctoral dissertation awards for my work on flow in elite athletes. I had enjoyed my time as a grad student in the US and also felt a pull to return home to Australia. I had also enjoyed researching more than I had anticipated, having originally embarked on graduate studies because of my interest in the growing field of applied sport psychology. I was faced with two attractive job offers upon the completion of my PhD: a sport psychology internship at the United States Olympic Training Center (USOC) in Colorado or an academic position back in Melbourne, Australia. It was one of many sliding door moments in my life. The attraction of returning to Australia eventually won out, and homeward bound I was.

Writing *Flow in Sports*

University life in Australia was not as rewarding an experience as I had hoped. Being several years behind North America in the sport psychology field at the time, I found within academic circles in Australia little awareness around flow. I became a silo researcher, and while I did engage in some interesting research projects, life as an academic in Australia was, for me, a mostly unrewarding experience. Interest in my work on flow came mostly from international colleagues, researchers, and students, enabling me to maintain a strong interest in flow despite the lack of support for my work in Australia. I also continued to enjoy the research and writing projects I was engaged in. Then, in 1997, a wonderful writing opportunity came my way.

I was spending part of a university sabbatical at the University of Chicago, working with and learning from Mike. A conversation with a sport psychology professor turned publishing company director, Rainer Martens, developed into a book contract with his company, Human Kinetics. Rainer understood flow and also understood the high profile of Mihaly Csikszentmihalyi and was pleased to have a contract with Mike on board. I was beyond pleased and also a little nervous. It was my first book, and I was in awe of Mike's writing, having read each of his books with a keen interest. The breadth and depth of Mike's knowledge came through in his book writing, and I knew I had been given the opportunity of a lifetime.

Writing *Flow in Sports* was a project that took place primarily by email, with my imminent return to Australia following my sabbatical. After we agreed on an outline, I'd write a draft chapter and email it across to Mike for his input. I'd then rework the chapter, Mike and I would fine-tune it, and then turn our attention to the subsequent chapter. Progress was sometimes good, sometimes slow. News of having my first child on its way hastened our efforts along. I set a goal of finishing a complete draft before the birth and got to appreciate first-hand the value of clear goals, a pre-condition for flow! The mission was accomplished, and the draft went to the editor before my son, Jack, arrived in late November 1998.

Writing *Flow in Sports* with Mike was a highlight of this part of my career. I am forever grateful for this opportunity I had to learn so directly from a thinker and writer who has helped shape understanding of what the experience of living a meaningful life is.

Mike and I had a similar motivation in writing *Flow in Sports*. We both enjoyed sport, and we recognized how sport provides a perfect playground in which to explore flow concepts. Mike had included a focus on the sport of basketball in his first book on flow, *Beyond Boredom and Anxiety*. And in his bestselling *Flow: The Psychology of Optimal Experience*, he wrote about various forms of movement and flow. Mike enjoyed being outdoors and would write to me about his adventures on their ranch in Montana, where he and his wife Isabella spent many happy summers.

Work and Flow

It would be almost ten years until I would see Mike in person following my 1997 visit to the University of Chicago. By this time, Mike had moved to Claremont Graduate University in California. I received an invitation to speak at a conference on flow sponsored by Nissan and held at the Stanford School of Medicine. Mike was the keynote speaker. Nissan was interested in how to design the interior of their cars to facilitate flow experience in driving. A team of mostly Japanese-speaking engineers sat on one side of the boardroom and a group of flow researchers on the other. I'm not entirely sure how much the Nissan team took from the conference discussions, but I enjoyed the opportunity to connect with Mike and other flow researchers.

Following the conference, my family and I visited Mike at his home in Claremont. I witnessed Mike engage my two young sons, aged eight and six at the time, with the same interest and curiosity that he brought to his own life. As he showed us around his home, Mike would bring interesting artifacts he had acquired from his travels from around the world to the attention of my sons. I watched as these moments of pure engagement unfolded between my boys and Mike.

The next and last time I would see Mike in person was several years later when he was a keynote speaker at a conference in Sydney in 2014. I sat in the audience and enjoyed listening to Mike speak to an auditorium filled with mostly laypeople, keen to hear Mike talk about his take on happiness. Despite his profile as a world-leading researcher in positive psychology, Mike had no pretense about him. He dressed casually and took audience questions with interest. I enjoyed a brief personal catch-up with Mike during a break in the conference. I did not know at the time that this would be the last time I would see him in person.

My career focus from 2007 shifted from academia to practicing as a psychologist in the sport and performance realms. This brings me full circle to a key reason I first undertook graduate training in sport psychology: to help people develop psychological skills for the challenges they face. I've found this work to be more rewarding than academia, although I do miss the research investigative process and writing about flow (hence this book). Working with clients to help them clarify their goals and develop strategies for their challenges was rewarding, as was sharing the flow concept with them. Clients were often not initially aware of what flow was, but invariably, once prompted with cues of what it is like to be in flow, they would have the 'aha' moment of connecting experiences they'd had when fully absorbed by an activity. Helping people to focus on the best moments in their chosen activity and working with them on developing strategies for facilitating optimal performances *and* experiences has been a positive career move for me.

My renewed interest in working with clients on understanding and accessing flow led me to think about writing a second book. I would have loved to have worked with Mike again, but this was not to eventuate, despite Mike and I having discussed the idea of writing a second edition to *Flow in Sports*. Mike remained very busy right up to his retirement, and then, in his latter years, he experienced some health challenges. My contact with him became sporadic. When emails did come in, Mike continued to express enthusiasm for life, their Montana summer home, their international travels, and his work at Claremont. Mike was always interested to hear about how my two sons were developing, including their achievements in the sport of men's artistic gymnastics. Mike embodied his work—always interested, curious, and engaged with what he was doing and who he was communicating with.

It was a very sad day when I learned of Mike's passing on October 20, 2021, at the age of 87. I had connected with him just a year earlier in an online meeting organized by long-term collaborator and friend Gary Gute (TheFlowChannel.com) in recognition and honor of Mike's 86th Birthday. In the next chapter, I share how Mike was remembered by some people who had the opportunity to work closely with him. Their perceptions highlight the significance of Mike's work and the way in which he lived what he studied. In sharing Mike's story, there are lessons for all of us about living in flow, that special place beyond boredom and anxiety.

CHAPTER 2

Remembering Mike and What He Taught Us About Flow

People were drawn to Mike from all corners of the world for his creativity, his insight into the human condition, his preference for studying assets rather than deficits, and his ability to make academic writing truly engaging.

—*Jennifer Schmidt, former student of Csikszentmihalyi*[1]

Early Influences

There are many accounts of the life trajectory of Mihaly Csikszentmihalyi, or Mike. He grew up in Italy, the son of Hungarian-born parents. He experienced World War II and was touched by the holocaust. However, when he reflected on that time, he always said his family didn't directly suffer too much compared to others, due to the diplomatic status of his father.[2] The origin of Mike's interest in flow dated all the way back to his childhood, before he had a name for the experience.

Observing the terrible impact of war around him, Mike wrote that chess provided a mental escape for him. Even then, he could perceive how his experience of chess differed depending on the skill of his opponent, an important observation that would eventually lead him to develop his flow model.

> *. . . as a ten-year-old I saw the whole world I took for granted crumbling. I realized, however, that when I played chess, I completely forgot what was going on,*

and for hours I had a great time. I felt completely involved, my mind was working, I had to be alert, and I had to process information about what was happening. I didn't have any chance to be distracted or any chance to worry about anything. I also noticed then that if I played against somebody really good, it wasn't much fun. If I played against somebody who played badly, it wasn't fun either because I started getting distracted and thinking about other things. But if my opponent was somebody in my own range of abilities, then the game was fun.[3]

In addition to chess, Mike loved to read. However, he was not enamored with traditional classroom learning. His own reading led him to an interest in psychology and eventually prompted his move to the USA as a young adult to study in this area. He came to the US without any material possessions, and having just witnessed in Europe the devastation that war brought to people's lives, he was motivated by wanting to help people improve their quality of life. This was to become a foundational motivation behind his work in psychology.

An interview by Izabela Lebuda with Mike in 2017 shed light on a step he took during his early teaching career that was to have a big impact on his subsequent development of the psychological concept of flow.[4] In a class he was teaching in 1968-69, he offered a range of possible study areas to his students to choose among, and they chose the topic of play. He asked his students to observe adults engaging in play and to ask these adults to describe what it felt like when they were doing their chosen activity. Mike was surprised to find that despite the difference in activities, whether sports, music, or games, the descriptions contained similar themes: liking the challenge or enjoying the development of their skill and the positive feedback they received about how they were doing during the activity. A couple of years later, Mike's research into flow as a psychological concept was ready for its public introduction.

Bypassing Boredom and Anxiety at a Young Age

As a young child, I did not see my whole world crumble around me as Mike described experiencing in the time of war that he grew up in. However, as Mike did with becoming immersed in chess, I similarly found ways in which to absorb myself, which became an escape from growing up in a home filled with family conflict. I remember, as a young child, spending many hours alone at home. I created simple games to play by myself. One was a memory game involving placing a collection of small objects on a large tray, covering the tray with a piece of material, and challenging myself to remember what each item was and where it was positioned on the tray.

My favorite activity was to use my large backyard as the setting for multiple iterations of an obstacle course. I'd use whatever outside objects I could find to create a challenging course, and I'd place them in various positions in the backyard. Every obstacle course I developed involved climbing large trees in my backyard and sometimes also climbing the six-foot fence to my neighbor's backyard, which at its far end included a small bushland of tall trees that I'd weave in and out of. Once my obstacle course was established, I'd then use a stopwatch to time myself on it, and over subsequent rounds, I'd set a goal of beating my previous time. It was a fun way to spend an afternoon by myself, and over 50 years later, I can remember that backyard, the trees I climbed up and jumped out of, and the enjoyment of these personal challenges. I guess, in hindsight, I was drawn to flow experience from a very early age! Ever since creating these challenges for myself as a young child, I have always found ways to avoid boredom in my life. When I read *Beyond Boredom and Anxiety* as a young adult, I could see how my life-long involvement in sport and physical activity was motivated by the enjoyable experience of finding that sweet spot between boredom and anxiety.

Mike Brings the Flow Framework to the World

In *Beyond Boredom and Anxiety*, published in 1975, Mike first wrote about his ideas on flow for a popular audience. He described flow in chess masters, composers, rock climbers, basketball players, dancers, and surgeons. It was the beginning of describing flow and introducing flow research to the world, and for me, it was one of the most important books I'd read. It set me on my lifelong course of work in flow as a researcher and psychologist.

Mike's next book on flow, *Optimal Experience* (1988), was a collaboration with his wife, Isabella. *Optimal Experience* was a compiled and edited volume of flow studies from around the world, including studies based on a novel approach to real-time data collection developed by Mike and one of his doctoral students, Reed Larson. This approach to data collection was called the Experience Sampling Method, or ESM, and it provided a way to tap into thoughts and feelings as participants were taking part in the various activities of their day.[5] It was an innovative development for collecting psychological data in the 1980s. Participants wore pagers for a week (the method predated mobile phones) that went off randomly over the course of the day, which prompted the individuals to record what they were doing and how they felt while doing it. The ESM became a mainstay of many of the research efforts of Mike and colleagues, and it is still used today but enhanced by the technology of mobile phones and apps.

Mike didn't rely only on ESM for his research. He continued to interview people to understand their flow experiences and accomplishments. For example, in his book *Creativity*, published in 1996, Mike shared what he learned about the creative process from interviewing exceptional people, including Nobel Prize winners, from many walks of life. In *Creativity*, flow is the framework from which Mike interpreted common patterns in creative processes and motivations of leaders in their domain, including physicists, biologists, poets, artists, and business leaders. Mike followed up this book with one focused on finding flow in the more mundane realm of everyday life. This book, *Finding Flow: The Psychology of Engagement with Everyday Life*, was published in 1997.

In the 2000s, Mike explored flow at work in-depth, collaborating with Howard Gardner and William Damon to write *Good Work: When Excellence and Ethics Meet*. Mike then went on to write another book focused on flow in work, *Good Business: Leadership, Flow, and the Making of Meaning* (2003). Mike consistently found in his flow research that work was one of the main activities in which people reported experiencing several characteristics of flow—except for wanting to be doing the activity!

These are some of Mike's many books, all of which illustrate his motivation to foster widespread understanding of the flow experience. Rather than just conducting academic research, Mike wanted as many people as possible to understand flow. His books were well-received, as was his work as an academic psychologist. In addition, Mike became an international speaker and consultant for corporations, schools, and non-profits.

Mike has been recognized as one of the eminent psychologists of the modern era.[6] One of his notable academic papers was a co-authored article published in 2000 with Martin Seligman where they overviewed the emerging field of positive psychology. In the special issue of *American Psychologist*, Seligman and Csikszentmihalyi situate flow as a central concept within one of the identified pillars of positive psychology: positive subjective experience.[7]

The Impact of Mike's Work Described by People Who Knew Him Well

As I re-read over several of the many obituaries about Mike in the writing of this book, consistent themes were apparent. Acclaim for his immense contribution to the fields of psychology and social science, and in particular for his critical role in the development of positive psychology. Known as the Father of Flow, he was praised for how he gave a language to this state of effortless focus and an explanation for its occurrence or absence. I had the opportunity to interview a couple of people very close to Mike for this book and will share some of their perceptions from having been among his long-term collaborators. They explain what Mike contributed to the global research community, as well as to the individual well-being of people from all walks of life.

Professor Antonella Delle Fave has had a life-long career as an academic at the University of Milan Medical School and was a long-term colleague of Mike's. I really enjoyed my conversation with Antonella and her passion for flow. The perspective Antonella provided on what Mike contributed with the development of his flow concept is an important voice to understanding Mike's work.

Antonella met Mike in 1981 when he visited the University of Milan at the invitation of an academic there who would become another important collaborator, Fausto Massimini. Fausto was researching flow in the context of biocultural evolution. It was Fausto and one of his graduate students at the time, Massimo Carli, who developed the first iteration of the eight-channel model of subjective experience (which you will see described in detail in Chapter 4). This model visually represents quality of experience and the correlating psychological states, which are defined by different ratios of challenges and skills.[8] This eight-channel model emerged from Mike's initial depiction of flow, which argued that quality of experience was predicated on the relationship between challenges and skills. This was the model that gave rise to the name of his first book on flow, *Beyond Boredom and Anxiety*.

Fausto and Antonella would go on to make significant contributions to the understanding of flow through their research spanning several decades. Antonella shared with me that Fausto, now retired, never stops saying that flow is one of the most important contributions to psychology in the twentieth century.

Moving from a place of being unaware of flow to recognizing it as a valued personal experience has a lot to do with language. One of the methods of introducing flow used by Mike, Antonella, and others (myself included) is to share quotes from people who describe being in flow. In what is known as the Flow Questionnaire, Mike and other researchers after him would share quotes, such as the one below, to help people tap into their own experience of the flow state:

> *My mind isn't wandering. I am not thinking of something else. I am totally involved in what I am doing.*[9]

Quotes such as this describe several of the standout features of being in flow, and when exposed to these statements, people often experience the "aha" moment of recognizing flow. Antonella shared that with the medical and health students she teaches at the University of Milan, silence descends into the lecture room when she reads out quotes like the one above, and she can feel people thinking. Some students experience a kind of epiphany, which can be observed in a change in gaze and facial expression. Once understood, flow can then be described in more detail. Mike provided this detail with the nine dimensions of flow, which I describe in the next chapter.

Antonella explained that despite its accessibility as a recognizable experience, flow is a complex psychological phenomenon. This inherently raises measurement challenges. To try to get around these challenges, some researchers have studied flow in laboratory settings, mostly using computer gaming as the focus activity. To measure challenge-skill balance, computer gaming researchers have used game difficulty as the proxy for challenge. Antonella pointed out, however, that difficulty level is not the same as challenge level, which in the flow model is a subjective perception tied in with motivation and perceptions of personal meaning. When measured in experimental settings, including examination of possible activity in the brain, it is important, Antonella argues, to recognize that the complex psychological experience of flow is probably not fully captured.

It's important to recognize that any measurement of flow is going to be only a partial reflection of the phenomenon. In our conversations, Antonella and I discussed Mike's premise that it's always a worthwhile endeavor to further our knowledge through whatever scientific means are available, but it is also important to recognize that research can only provide a partial picture of the flow experience. The holistic, global experience that flow is can perhaps best be understood when we experience it in the body.

How do we experience flow in the body? What happens at the physiological level? Antonella has written about flow as a state of moderate mental effort associated with increased parasympathetic modulation of sympathetic activity.[10] Put more simply, it is a state of both relaxation and excitement where one experiences effortless concentration. A paradox? This is exactly how Mike described flow, as an experience involving apparent paradoxes. For example, being in control without trying to control and concentrating deeply without perceived effort. It is uniting these paradoxes that make flow the unique and memorable experience that it is.

Understanding Flow by Understanding the Father of Flow

Mike can be regarded as somewhat of a paradox himself when one tries to categorize him into a particular discipline. While he is often referred to as a psychologist, Antonella shared how she viewed him not as a psychologist but rather as a thinker. One who had a view of science as a whole. Antonella argued that his vision of human experience, of which flow is a central part, cannot be framed solely as psychology, saying:

> *You can't imprison a worldview into a discipline. I think the picture provided by Mike was an existential picture of flow.*

As a thinker herself, Antonella saw Mike as not only working across multiple disciplines but also continuously asking himself questions. And one of the most important questions Mike was interested in asking was how to understand the human experience from a positive perspective. Having grown up in a time of war and witnessing how people who came through the war varied widely in their response—some developing great resilience, while others remained fragile and lost themselves—Mike became curious about finding meaning and enjoyment in life. He was actually way ahead of the official launch of positive psychology as an important branch of the field, heralded by the article he co-wrote with Seligman in American Psychologist in 2000.

In his final years, Mike was focused on bringing flow into the digital age, where anyone could access ideas about making flow relevant and practical in everyday life. He collaborated in the creation of the award-winning online simulation experience FLIGBY (Flow is Good Business for You) and the creation of TheFlowChannel.com.

Co-founders of The Flow Channel with Mike were Drs. Gary and Deanne Gute.[11] Gary and Deanne had spent many years getting to know Mike, first through his writings and then through the development of a personal friendship that began when Mike was a visiting professor at Iowa State University, where Gary and Deanne were both working on doctoral dissertations.

Gary and Deanne shared with me how Mike was both proud of and humbled by the extent to which flow took off as a scientific concept. He was always excited to learn about how individuals and organizations were using flow experience to enhance quality of life in practical ways. One application of his work that Gary and Deanne knew Mike was particularly excited about was how the theory and research on flow could be applied to improve systems. For example, applying flow in business to improve job design, and to improve the meaning and enjoyment that people could find in their work.

When I asked Gary about his understanding of Mike's perceptions of how flow was being presented in his later years, Gary said that while Mike was happy with the ever-growing interest in flow, he did not appreciate what, at times, was an oversimplification of this experience. For example, some people working with flow in the applied arena would use terms like a flow "switch" or "hacking" the flow state. Gary shared Mike's perception that this over-simplification does a disservice to the complexity of flow. Gary stated that Mike viewed flow as something that is possible for all of us but that it only results after a lot of hard work: developing a high level of skill, facing challenges, and figuring out how to master those challenges. It's an ongoing process. It can take a long time to get to the point where you're able to experience flow easily.

I liked how Gary summed up the importance of flow:

> *While flow is not a simple antidote to all of our woes, it does provide a powerful framework that allows individuals and systems to function at their best. By recognizing the importance of living an authentic life that values challenge, and attention, and the intrinsic motivation that results from working toward meaningful goals.*

I met Gary and Deanne for the first time online in October 2020, when they hosted a celebration on Zoom in honor of Mike's 86th birthday. I learned about this via a Flow Channel Facebook post on the day of the event, and I dropped everything to have an opportunity to see and speak to Mike again. It was wonderful to see Mike join in on the online 86th birthday celebration that Gary and Deanne organized in his honor, coinciding with a panel discussion of flow in rock climbing, painting, and farming. I didn't know at the time that this was to be the last time I would see Mike alive before his death, just after his 87th birthday in 2021. I noticed in Mike in this online event the same curiosity and interest that I had observed in him all those years ago when I first took the step of reaching out to ask him about flow.

When I asked Gary and Deanne to describe Mike as a person in our interview, the first words they used were *curiosity* and *complexity*. The other words and phrases they used to describe Mike identified qualities that I was also very familiar with from having spent time with him: humility, being a great conversationalist, and being a great observer—Deanne commented that you could see him just silently observing and taking everything in any time you would spend time with him. I remember this clearly when I spent time with Mike—you could observe him thinking.

Deanne recounted how meeting Mike totally defied expectations of what an evening with an important psychologist and thinker would be like. He was a rare combination of vast, interconnected knowledge and humility. During a dinner with Mike, weighty ideas one minute would give way to Mike joking and storytelling. He always appreciated the most simple, everyday pleasures, such as a good meal and glass of wine.

Lived Complexity

Gary and Deanne shared many examples of Mike living by the values he professed. They describe Mike as compassionate and honest, and a term Gary used that really resonated with me was "lived complexity."

As Gary explained, Mike embodied the psychological complexity he wrote about. He was someone who could, in his thinking and in his behavior, embrace and practice the presence of opposites. Gary commented that oftentimes, someone who is comfortable embracing and practicing opposites can be perceived as not being able to make up their mind, or not being consistent, or perhaps being ambivalent. Gary said that Mike couldn't care less about that perception because he truly felt that there was wisdom and value in appreciating opposites, including convergent and divergent thinking, introversion and extraversion, playfulness and seriousness of purpose, traditionalism and iconoclasm, and more.

Antonella reflected on the rare open-mindedness Mike displayed. She believes it may be his life experiences that had the most to do with shaping his complex approach to life and work. As a young person, Mike moved many times, from a part of Italy that now belongs to Croatia, to summers in Budapest, to Rome, and then as a young adult, to the United States. His family upbringing exposed him to diversity. The war brought economic hardship and loss for the family, and above all, according to Antonella, "the relativity of belonging":

> *The contextual relativity of not really belonging to one community probably led him to see things with an open-mindedness that belongs to people who have experienced many different contexts.*

Mike described in depth how complexity in consciousness comes about through the intentional development of the opposite qualities of differentiation and integration. Differentiation and integration are described in more detail in later sections of this book, but briefly, they refer, respectively, to becoming more uniquely yourself and integrating with the society in which you live. The balance of these opposites gives us more opportunities for flow. Each flow experience helps us develop our capacities and gives us more options for action in the world. This is complexity in the best sense of the word.

As a result of the Facebook birthday celebration event for Mike in 2020, I got to learn more about The Flow Channel. One outcome of having developed this online presence is the opportunity provided to Gary and Deanne to continue promoting Mike's work. They described how they are developing The Flow Channel into a Foundation. In our interview, Deanne described the purpose of the Foundation: To develop a flow fellowship focused on helping humanity thrive by advancing the science and practical psychology of Mike's work. Basically, Deanne and Gary are committed to building on the gifts that Mike's legacy has provided us with. In Gary's words, they owe Mike a debt of gratitude for his kindness and generosity as a mentor, friend, and collaborator. They are also committed to sharing the tremendous value flow can bring to the world and to the quality of life for future generations. Mike believed that this was the ultimate purpose of understanding flow: using it to contribute to the positive evolution of relationships and systems.

A Life Well Lived

Everyone who knew Mike well had similar recollections in describing Mike as a person. Curiosity, a focus on positivity, humility, warmth, generosity of spirit, and a definite stance of listening in a non-judgmental way. On his passing, colleagues and former students praised Mike's generous and yet humble spirit. He made anyone in his presence feel comfortable and offered encouragement to countless colleagues, students, authors, and strangers looking to soak up his wisdom and receive feedback on their ideas.

Someone else who knew all this very well was his colleague and co-founder of the Quality of Life Research Center at Claremont Graduate University, Jeanne Nakamura. Jeanne remarked in a University of Chicago newspaper tribute to Mike on his passing that he was the best example of all the things that he taught us about the life well lived.[12] Higher praise would be difficult to give, especially from the person who worked alongside him for probably the longest time.

I had the opportunity to meet Jeanne Nakamura during my sabbatical with Mike and found her to be both very hard-working, and also a wonderful right-hand person to support Mike's work at the University of Chicago. During my sabbatical, I also got to meet other doctoral students of Mike and saw in them a similar loyalty to their advisor that I witnessed in Jeanne. I observed this loyalty not just in former graduate students but also in collaborators of Mike with whom I got to connect.

When I asked Gary how he first learned about flow, he explained that it had actually come about with an experience somewhat similar to my own in the way we both stumbled upon Mike's wisdom in one of his books. Though the book was different, Gary's first reading of Mike's 1990 *Flow* had the same impact as my reading of *Beyond Boredom and Anxiety*. Gary commented that when he first got in touch with Mike, he wrote to him with trepidation. In response, he received a great gift in Mike's enthusiastic response to his research ideas. Gary didn't expect this prestigious professor to actively engage with him, helping him to shape his dissertation, and serving on his dissertation committee. Just as he had been with me, Mike was a responsive and enthusiastic presence as Gary developed his research.

I'm reminded of another one of Mike's doctoral students, Jennifer Schmidt, who shared in a University of Chicago newspaper tribute to Mike that she saw Mike's work as being *"like a flashlight in a dark tunnel."*[13] I think this is the perfect description of what Mike accomplished by introducing the world to the concept of flow.

Speaking with Gary and Deanne Gute, Antonella Delle Fave, and others shed light on who Mike was as a thinker, scientist, and as a human being. Their perceptions underscored the positive way in which I had experienced Mike in the precious time I got to spend with him. For me, when I think about the question of what stands out most about Mike, it is his unfathomably brilliant way of seeing the world, how we can best live in the period of time given to us, and how we can best confront the unknowns of the future. In the remainder of this book, I share with you the practical aspects of the flow framework that will help you be like Mike, living your best life.

CHAPTER 3

So, What Is Flow and How Do You Know It Is Flow?

When you're on a climb and the moves feel easier than you expected them to, and your body is moving up the wall in an automatic way, and you're completely present. There's no other thoughts going through your mind. It's basically just like you and the rock. And you're constantly kind of surprised that you're doing everything so well, but also feel super in control, like you could kind of do anything. And then when you get to the top, or whatever happens next, you kind of pop out of this bubble, and you feel really ecstatic. And on top of the world. And you will probably never forget those experiences.

—Hazel Findlay, leading female rock climber

Understanding Flow

Rock climber Hazel Findlay, in the opening quote above, describes how she experiences flow. She shared this description with me when discussing how she would help another climber to understand flow. In addition to being a world-class climber herself, Hazel is a coach to climbers. A big part of her work is helping the people she works with to change their relationship with fear and anxiety and to access flow. You will hear more from Hazel in upcoming chapters.

Flow is fun; flow is freedom. F-L-O-W: what a great name for when everything comes together, and you experience life at optimal. How did the name flow come to be? When Mike interviewed people about their experiences when fully engaged in what they were doing, these artists, athletes, chess players, and surgeons referred to things *flowing* or having a sense of *flow* as they worked. The term "flow" captures well the experience of being effortlessly carried along with one's endeavor.

Even though a chess player planning their next move uses different specific skills than a surgeon mid-procedure, the experiences of people in different domains such as these have been reliably shown to be remarkably similar. I will outline these defining characteristics of flow in an upcoming section.

I experienced flow before I had a name for the experiences. These were the times, mostly in sport, when my performance went to the next level. Where fun and freedom came alive. My perception of time changed, mostly the sense that it was standing still. Focusing was easy, and the monkey mind was nowhere to be seen.

Each time I experienced flow, I had another moment to put in my memory book. But I did not connect these experiences at the time. I saw them as happening somewhat outside of the "me" I usually brought to performance. The slightly over-involved me, wanting to do well but not always believing in myself when pressure was felt. When flow was present, worry about my performance was absent, and even more liberating, so were the thinking and analyzing parts of my mind.

It would be many experiences later, many years later, that I reached for *Beyond Boredom and Anxiety* on the University of Illinois bookshelves. I was then able to put a name to these seemingly random, formerly disconnected experiences.

The flow experience has been defined by Mike as comprising nine characteristics. As part of my PhD on the flow experience in elite athletes, I examined athletes' descriptions of being in flow from the perspective of these nine dimensions. The descriptions fit Csikszentmihalyi's nine-dimensional flow model well. This was not an isolated finding. Across research conducted in many different settings and in different cultures around the world, there is remarkable consistency in the experience of flow. I'll set out what these key components of the flow experience are next.

The Nine Dimensions of Flow

The first three of the nine dimensions have come to be known as the *pre-conditions* for flow. That is, when these three factors are met, the stage is set for flow.

1. A balance between challenges and skills

This characteristic is key to understanding that flow is an accessible experience. Mike described flow as occurring when you are in a situation of high challenge, and you have the skills to (just) meet the challenge:

> *Flow tends to occur when a person's skills are fully involved in overcoming a challenge that is just about manageable.*[1]

Remembering that this is a psychological model, what matters more is not the objective level of challenge or skill but rather your belief in your skills, your perception of the challenge, and what the challenge means to you. For example, Andrew, an Australian rugby union player playing in a World Cup final, shared with me his perspective on this major challenge: *"Guess it was the extreme challenge, but we didn't approach it as a major hurdle."*

The challenge-skill balance is how Mike operationally defined flow, making it the most important pre-condition, or pre-requisite, for flow. The challenge-skill balance dimension is so important to understanding flow and to understanding how flow is accessible, that the next chapter is focused on detailing how challenges and skills are predicted to interact in the flow model to determine quality of experience.

2. Clear goals

Having clear goals is about knowing what it is you are going to do every step of the way in a performance or activity. Moment by moment, you know what is expected of you and what you want to do in the situation. The goals are process goals, guiding what you are actually doing in the performance. We are not talking here about outcome goals, which have to do with the final results or outcome of your performance. The clear goals dimension of flow is about the clarity of purpose that occurs when we bring ourselves fully to the task. Sometimes, this translates to a finely tuned sense of anticipation, such as described to me by George, a football player: *"There was one stage when I went up to catch a ball, and I knew when he kicked it, I was going to catch it."*

3. Immediate feedback

Feedback is continuously received, so you know whether you are on track to reach your goals. The feedback is clear and immediate and allows you to stay connected to your performance. Feedback can come from a variety of sources. Most important is the feedback you receive from your body or the actions you take. Paying attention to this internal feedback keeps you connected to your performance. However, valuable feedback can also come from external sources, such as a coach, teammate, parent, or friend. In flow, feedback is easy to receive and act upon and is linked with the process goals of the preceding dimension. For example, Simon, a successful international road cyclist, shared with me some of the key sources of feedback he was focused on during an important race:

> *What gear you're riding; what position you're sitting in; where the second, third, fourth, and fifth riders are sitting in the bunch. What numbers are in the breakaway; how many riders there are in front of you—all these things take your attention.*

By focusing on these specific sources of feedback, Simon was able to stay totally connected to his performance and performance goals. Sport is a great environment for experiencing flow because of several factors, including that it provides participants with clear and immediate feedback. Other flow facilitative factors include that sport is a well-structured activity with graded levels of challenge, and where there is a specific set of skills to develop at each stage or progression. The rules of the game or event mean that we can have clear goals about what we're trying to achieve. And during the activity, we can receive clear feedback that lets us know whether we are on track with our goals. Sometimes, we're not listening to our bodies or paying attention to our environment. But when we are paying attention to what the environment and our actions are telling us, so that we keep focused on our goals, and we meet the challenge with trust in our skills, we have set the stage to achieve flow.

To understand what happens in flow, we turn now to the six characteristics that describe this experience:

4. A sense of actions and awareness becoming one

Merging of action-awareness is what Mike called this dimension. What happens here is that you're so involved in what you're doing that you aren't thinking about yourself as separate from what you're doing. You and the performance interconnect to such an extent that no separation is experienced between the two. You might hear athletes describe how they felt like their equipment seemed to be an extension of their body, so connected are they to what they are doing. For example, Simon, the cyclist, describes the bike and himself feeling like one machine:

> *It doesn't seem as if you're sitting on a bike. You feel altogether like it's just one piece of machinery working together... like you're part of this machine that you were born with, and it's how you move.*

A musician may sense the same sort of oneness with their instrument. The actor is not just speaking the words of their part but rather embodying the character. The next flow dimension, total concentration, helps us to understand how this merging of action and awareness can occur.

5. Total concentration

This is perhaps the clearest feature of being in flow—a total engagement in the task at hand. Your concentration is completely on the task as you perform it. There is no mental energy left to put attention on anything else. Nor does one seek to do so when experiencing this level of total absorption since the experience is a positive change from the usual split attention that we bring to most tasks. The level of connection to our activity leads to the sense of being one with what we are doing, as described in the section on action-awareness merging. This total focus is also connected to the flow dimensions that follow, and the centrality of total concentration to flow is thus not surprising. Mike referred to the dimension of total concentration as the "signature quality" of flow.[2]

When describing the centrality of concentration to flow, Mike and his colleague Jeanne Nakamura emphasized that the type of attentional focus in flow is qualitatively different from attention outside of flow. They referred to this flow concentration as effortless attention and described it thus:

> *There is a phenomenological difference between subjective experience when full attention is effortful and when it is effortless, and we hypothesize that it is specifically the experience of complete but also effortless attention that is associated with being in the enjoyable state of flow.*[3]

Through their data collection method that tapped into subjective experience as it was occurring, the Experience Sampling Method (ESM), it was possible to examine how people felt about fully concentrating when it was hard to do so—versus effortlessly concentrating. Mike and Jeanne found that all the other flow dimensions described in this chapter were connected with effortless attention but not with *effortful* attention. They pointed out that we can improve the quality of our life experience by learning how to engage effortless attention for the tasks we have to do in everyday life. We will visit ways of improving our skill in engaging effortless attention as I continue describing the dimensions of flow and in a later chapter on mastery.

Another difference in the quality of attentional focus in flow (compared with when not in flow) is that there is no room in one's mind for anything other than the task at hand. I came across a unique way of describing what happens when concentration is completely on a task. The movie critic and historian Roger Ebert wrote:

> *I find that when I am actually writing, I enter a zone of concentration too small to admit my troubles.*[4]

I love this description of not having space for one's troubles when totally focused on a task. It depicts how complete concentration can overcome worry about whether what one is engaged in is working or worry about what others might be thinking of you. This lack of concern about possible failure and other people's perceptions set us up for the next two dimensions of flow—sense of control (#6) and loss of self-consciousness (#7).

6. Sense of control

The feeling of being in control is an interesting one when we are in flow. Control is not sought after but is also not questioned. The feeling is like one can do no wrong, as described by Simon, the cyclist:

> *You feel like there's nothing that will be able to stop you or get in your way. And you're ready to tackle*

> *anything, and you don't fear any possibility*
> *happening, and it's just exhilarating.*

The absence of fear facilitates engagement in the high challenge of the task. Mike initially called this dimension the paradox of control because control was felt despite not being a sought-after experience. There's a great quote from Michael Jordan about how he perceived the basketball court during a game as peaceful—a paradox in itself on first appearances. As Jordan described,

> *The basketball court for me during a game is the most*
> *peaceful place I can imagine. On the basketball court,*
> *I worry about nothing. When I'm out there, no one*
> *can bother me.*[5]

When you are totally focused with attention solely on the task in front of you, there is no room for fear of things not working out. Similarly, there is no room for worry about how one is being perceived, the next flow dimension.

7. Loss of self-consciousness

This dimension makes flow a liberating experience for the otherwise preoccupied self. During flow, concern for oneself drops away. You aren't preoccupied with what others may be thinking of you. We spend a lot of time worrying about how others perceive us, and society reinforces this concern through systems of rewards for the person who achieves the most or looks the prettiest. To be free of concern for self allows for a more complete involvement in what we are doing. And it is from the complete involvement in the task that the freedom from self-consciousness can emerge.

The experience of groups or teams is helpful in explaining the loss of self-consciousness dimension of flow. When working as part of a group or team, the potential for flow is in many ways more difficult due to the need for cohesiveness in mental approach amongst all participating. However, being part of something larger than oneself can facilitate a loss of self-consciousness. And when there is a collective spirit of attention among all group members, a wonderful synergy can emerge. This synergy can be observed by audiences of sport, music, and other performing arts events and felt keenly by the participants.

Creative director Francisco Zamorano describes the experience of letting go of self-consciousness among a group of musicians:

> *Most musicians know about the unique state that is reached in the music sessions: You are not focused on yourself, you are focused on the collective action, on the others, on the music. Your self-consciousness is reduced, and the perception of the synergy generated as a group is enhanced.*[6]

8. Perceived difference in the passing of time

Time transforms in our perceptions when in flow. Sometimes the perception is that time speeds up; other times, a slowing down, as illustrated by Katie, a US national champion figure skater I interviewed:

> *Everything else goes away. It almost happens in slow motion, even though you're doing things at the correct time with the music and everything. Nothing else matters. It's just such an eerie, eerie feeling.*

Katie illustrates the link between time transformation and total focus—nothing else matters when we are absorbed without limits in what we are doing. Time may seem to slow down or speed up, depending on the nature of the task; or it may simply cease to exist in our perceptions for that time we are in flow.

In my research with athletes when I was examining the flow dimensions, I found that not all athletes reported perceptions of time passing differently. Mike also noted this and explained that sometimes time is part of the challenge. For example, in a race, an athlete seeks to perform in the shortest possible amount of time. Awareness of time is part of the goal, and feedback may center around time during the performance. It is less likely in such performances that an athlete will lose awareness of time. The same is no doubt true for other performers where time is part of the challenge. For example, an emergency medicine doctor performing a life-saving intervention may be relying on time as a critical source of feedback about the progress and next steps of the surgery.

While time transformation may not always be experienced, I have found that when it is, the reported level of flow is deep. The same is true for the loss of self-consciousness dimension of flow. Letting go of this sense of self-reflection is not easy for most of us to do. When we do, it is an indication we are deeply immersed in what we are doing. Deep immersion in a task or activity that is not time-dependent can bring about memorable flow experiences.

9. Enjoyment of the experience

Flow is inherently enjoyable in large part because of this preceding set of flow characteristics. Csikszentmihalyi called this intrinsic enjoyment the autotelic experience. Autotelic means engaging in an activity for the experience the activity provides. The word autotelic was derived from the Greek, 'auto' (self) and 'telic' (goal) and signifies an activity one does for the reward inherent in that activity.[7] Flow can thus be seen to become an important motivation for continued participation in an endeavor. So said an Olympic rower I interviewed, Pip:

> *Knowing that flow can happen keeps you going through all the bad rows or the not-so-good rows. It's just a little bit of magic.*

I recently saw Sir Paul McCartney play at a concert that was part of his 2023 world tour. At 81 years young, McCartney held the audience enraptured for three hours. And his energy levels did not falter. While his voice may not be as strong as it used to be, he sang his way effortlessly through hit after hit; his mastery of multiple instruments is still first-class, and his performance skills are impeccable. He has had 66 years of perfecting his craft, and thus, perhaps it is not surprising that his skills are outstanding.

What stood out for me during the concert was how much McCartney was enjoying himself. He engaged with the audience more than most rock concert performers I've experienced, and with an authenticity that suggested that his enjoyment is tied in with experiencing flow on stage. Several flow factors were evident in his performance: a lack of self-consciousness, effortless concentration, being in control on stage, and enjoying what he was doing—plus the mere fact of being on stage doing what he was doing at 81 years old demonstrated his attitude toward challenge. In an interview during the time of his recent live performances, McCartney said, *"Why would I retire? Sit at home and watch TV? No thanks. I'd rather be out playing."*

Flow as enjoyment

Mike would often use the words flow and enjoyment interchangeably. He viewed enjoyment as being intertwined with experiencing the characteristics of flow. Enjoyment was thus an active process and one where growth was experienced. Just as trying to produce flow is likely to lead one further away from the experience, seeking happiness without active engagement was likely to bear little fruit, according to Mike:

> *It is by being fully involved with every detail of our lives, whether good or bad, that we find happiness; not by trying to look for it directly.*[8]

Mike argued that enjoyment occurs when we accept the challenge in front of us:

> *Enjoyable events occur when a person has not only met some prior expectation or satisfied a need or desire, but also gone beyond what he or she has been programmed to do and achieved something unexpected, perhaps even unimagined before.*[9]

Enjoyment as flow is different from enjoyment as a positive affective state. Mike's definition is about finding or making meaning, stretching previous limits, and growing psychologically as a result. This way of defining enjoyment makes sense. If you reflect on times in your life when you have stretched your previous limits and achieved something meaningful, you probably view that experience as having been an enjoyable time.

Interestingly, other writers have drawn parallels between experiencing happiness and the flow state. One example is James Maddux, writing about the relationships between happiness and positive affect. Maddux argued that the latter is achieved via experiencing flow:

> *Curiously and consistent with the assumptions of Eastern philosophies, it is this ability to become absorbed in whatever activity one is engaged in at the present moment; in other words, it is the capacity for experiencing flow.*[10]

Maddux's reasoning went like this: achieving flow leads to positive affect, and positive affect, in turn, predicts happiness. The interviews I have conducted with elite performers confirm the importance of flow experiences to the overall positive valence with which they view their participation.

Recognizing Flow

Flow occurs when some or all of the above nine dimensions co-arise in one's experience. In achievement settings, the challenge-skill balance is a key indicator of the quality of experience one will encounter. Challenges high and skills high set the stage for flow. Two points are important to understand this challenge-skill balance. First, the benchmarks for low, average, and high are individual. A high challenge for you is one that takes you beyond the average level of challenges you generally find in your activity.

Similarly, a high skill level is one above the average skill level needed to do your activity. Second, this balance of challenges and skills comes down to how you perceive the challenge and how you perceive your skills in relation to the challenge. This is particularly true at the upper end of achievement in a domain. For example, a widely held perception of Olympic athletes is that they are very confident in their skills. My research with many elite athletes, including those who have achieved the highest levels in their sport, is that confidence is far from solid. Athletes who compete at the highest levels of their sport do have extraordinary skills. However, the challenges can also be extraordinarily high—and many uncontrollable factors are encountered in the journey of being an elite athlete. Unless an athlete has an impenetrable mindset toward their performance, it is not difficult to understand how belief in one's skills can be called into question.

In recent years, I have worked in my psychology practice with medical doctors preparing for their specialty exams and specialists seeking to optimize their psychological skills for the demands of their practice. As with elite athletes, a common perception about medical doctors is that they are a group of not only highly skilled but also highly confident professionals. However, in a profession where the challenges are seemingly endless as one progresses through medical school into residency and then into specialty training programs, it is not surprising that doctors' belief in their skills is sometimes put to the test. And once practicing, doctors are held to very high expectations within the community to be faultless. A large part of my performance psychology consulting work with medical doctors is to help them trust their skills and accept feeling uncomfortable in the very demanding training and exam conditions they have to progress through, as well as when challenges inevitably arise in their practice of medicine.

If the pre-condition of challenge-skills balance is met, having a clear blueprint of what it is you are aiming to do in your performance helps facilitate flow via harnessing attention to the task. Tuning into the feedback that comes from your performance, as it occurs, helps keep the attention moving with the task. The role of attention cannot be over-emphasized. Flow is total concentration, and from this full focus comes other experiential characteristics of flow. For example, self-consciousness disappears because no mental energy is taken away from the task to preoccupation with how well one is doing in the eyes of others. The perception of time changes because of the total absorption in the task. There is no worry about control because worry has dropped off the radar. It is easy to see how such total engagement in a task creates a high level of enjoyment—this autotelic experience creates motivation to experience flow again. Simon, the highly successful road cyclist I interviewed, described to me that his main motivation to continue cycling was to re-experience flow:

> *There's nothing, there's no experience in sport that is as exhilarating or rewarding as being in flow. That's what makes me keep riding, knowing that I might get it again.*

In this chapter, I've described the nine dimensions of flow. Understanding flow through the detailed lens of these nine dimensions provides an in-depth picture of the experience. One thing to keep in mind when considering flow from this dimensional perspective is that flow is more than the sum of its parts. The nine flow dimensions are just that—qualities of the experience. It is the coming together of several, or all, of these dimensions that create an experience of flow. When working as an academic, I developed, with colleagues Herbert Marsh, Robert Eklund, and Andrew Martin, self-report scales designed to tap into the nine dimensions of flow and the overall experience of flow.[11] While we were aware that no measurement can capture the entirety of flow experience, the flow scales were developed to foster research examining flow and relationships between flow and other psychological concepts, such as self-confidence, anxiety, and motivation. In one research study, we found that athletes high in perceived ability experienced flow more frequently than athletes low in perceived ability and/or athletes high in anxiety.[12] Similar findings were obtained for relationships between flow and motivation, where intrinsic motivation was positively associated with flow experiences, while extrinsic motivation was not associated with flow.

I believe that a combination of quantitative and qualitative research will yield the most insights into flow, and as a researcher, I used both research approaches to investigate this experience. Qualitative data provided particularly rich descriptions of what it was like to experience flow. For example, this quote from Bethany, a US national champion figure skater I interviewed, demonstrates how flow is experienced as the simultaneous expression of its dimensions:

> *It was just one of those programs that clicked. I mean everything went right, everything felt good . . . it's just such a rush, like you feel it could go on and on and on; like you don't want it to stop because it's going so well. It's almost as though you don't have to think; it's like everything goes automatically without thinking. . . . it's like you're on automatic pilot, so you don't have any thoughts. You hear the music, but you're not aware that you're hearing it, because it is a part of it all.*[13]

There's no question this figure skater was experiencing flow. Her description provides a clear insight into what flow feels like while experiencing it. I've found that upon describing flow to people, an aha experience kicks in almost without exception. And just like what happened for me when I read *Beyond Boredom and Anxiety*, others now have a name for their times of highest enjoyment.

To better understand how flow can come about and what other subjective experiences are likely to occur when challenges and skills are not in alignment, I next describe the models Mike and colleagues have developed to describe flow and other psychological states.

CHAPTER 4

Understanding Flow Experience Through the Challenge-Skill Balance Model

Enjoyment appears at the boundary between boredom and anxiety, when the challenges are just balanced with the person's capacity to act.

—*Csikszentmihalyi*[1]

I love this description by Mike of how flow occurs at the boundary between boredom and anxiety, where challenges and skills are balanced, and both are extending the individual. The challenge-skill balance dimension is the first identified flow dimension for a reason. It is the operational definition of flow that Mike developed and worked from in his research. Mike considered the balance between a situation of high challenge and high skill to be a prerequisite for flow to occur. In his later research, Mike referred to the challenge-skill balance, along with clear goals and unambiguous feedback, as the three *pre-conditions* to flow, as described in the previous chapter.

Because the challenge-skill balance is so foundational to understanding if an experience will result in flow, this chapter describes how to assess experience through the lens of the relative balance of challenges and skills. In our book *Flow in Sports*, Mike and I coined the term *CS Balance* to denote finding a flow-facilitative balance between your perceived challenges and skills in a given situation.[2]

Challenges can be thought of as opportunities for action, and skills as the ability to act. The models that follow describe different subjective experiences that occur based on different ratios of challenges to skills.

The models are predicated on an individual's average level of challenge and average level of skill in a situation or task. When movement occurs away from one's average level of challenge or average level of skill, specific experiential states are predicted to occur. I'll overview these different psychological states next.

Models to Understand How Flow Occurs

I find the visual models depicting the intersection of challenges and skills to be particularly useful for aiding understanding of when flow can occur and also how flow relates to other subjective experiences. Figure 1 depicts an adaptation of the four-quadrant model that Mike and I used in our book, *Flow in Sports*. As demonstrated in Figure 1, experience is predicted to vary based on the relative balance of challenges and skills. And, as shown on the intersection between the vertical and horizontal axes on the graph, an individual's "average" level of challenge and skill in a situation is the baseline from which the experience of flow, or other subjective experience, is predicted to occur. Other subjective experiences in this model are *Anxiety*, *Apathy*, and what Mike and I termed *Relaxation-Boredom*. This lower left quadrant was initially called Boredom by Mike. However, over years of collecting data on how people perceived their experience when skills were higher than challenges, Mike concluded that the word Relaxation seemed to describe the experience best. Nonetheless, like all extended holidays where relaxation is the sole focus, an ongoing lack of challenge often eventually leads from relaxation to boredom. This move from relaxation to boredom is better illustrated in the eight-channel model of flow. Figure 2 illustrates this model, where there are eight different subjective experiences according to the relative ratio of challenge to skill in a situation. The right side of the model depicts positive subjective experiences. Nestled between *Relaxation* and *Flow* is the experience of *Control*. These three experiences, relaxation, flow, and control, are all positive ones. According to the model, a sense of control is experienced when skills are high and challenges moderately high. Most people gravitate to the experience of control in achievement situations. Feeling in control is sought after, as we feel competent and able to meet the demands of the situation. Confidence grows when we feel in control.

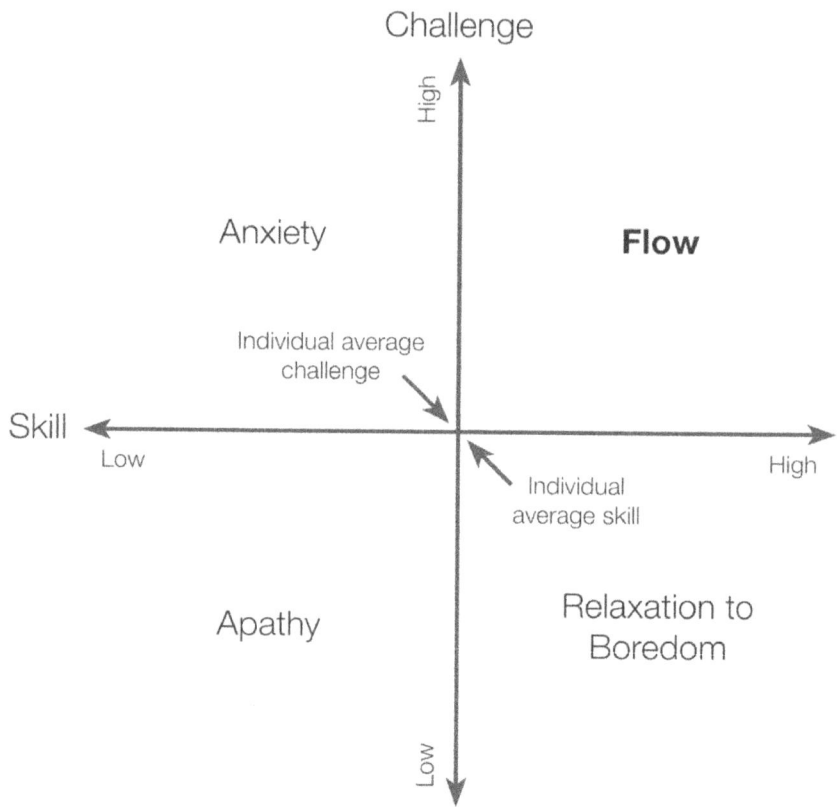

Figure 1. *Four-Quadrant Model of Subjective Experience*
Figure by Susan A. Jackson (2024). Adapted by permission, from Jackson and Csikszentmihalyi (1999),
p. 37, and Csikszentmihalyi and Csikszentmihalyi (1988), p. 261.[3]

To move from control to flow requires moving out of the comfort of feeling like we've got everything in our grasp, to a place where there is potential uncertainty. This can be understood by remembering that in the experience of control, perceived skills are slightly higher than challenges, meaning confidence is high. In the flow channel, challenges are slightly higher than skills, and hence, there's no longer the certainty of having everything within one's control.

The difference in quality of experience between control and flow is an interesting one. Skills, as illustrated in Figure 2, are perceived to be high in both experiences. The difference comes down to the relative level of challenge. Flow is high challenge, whereas control is a moderate level of challenge. There's more guarantee of success when in control. However, there is more opportunity for growth and extending prior limits if one can let go of control and be open to the higher challenge of flow. Mike explained (1997) that, like flow, control is a positive state, "*. . . where one feels happy, strong, satisfied. But one tends to lack concentration, involvement, and a feeling that what one does is important.*"[4] Increasing the challenge will lead to more involvement and to the possibility of attaining new levels of performance via experiencing flow.

If we keep moving counterclockwise in the model from flow to where challenges remain high, but skill level moves to being at a moderate level, the experience of high *Arousal* is predicted. A simple way to understand arousal in the sense in which it is being used here is to view it as anxiety without negative thoughts or worry arising. Our physiology is activated, perhaps with increased heart rate, butterflies in the stomach, increase in temperature, etc. What is absent are the negative emotions we tend to attach to these physiological changes we experience when in a high state of arousal. The challenge is perceived to be higher than our skill, but if we were to stretch our capabilities, we might meet the challenge. In this state of high arousal, one tends to feel mentally focused and engaged in what one is doing. The difference from flow in terms of how one feels, is that it's not so enjoyable an experience, and we feel a little bit out of control.

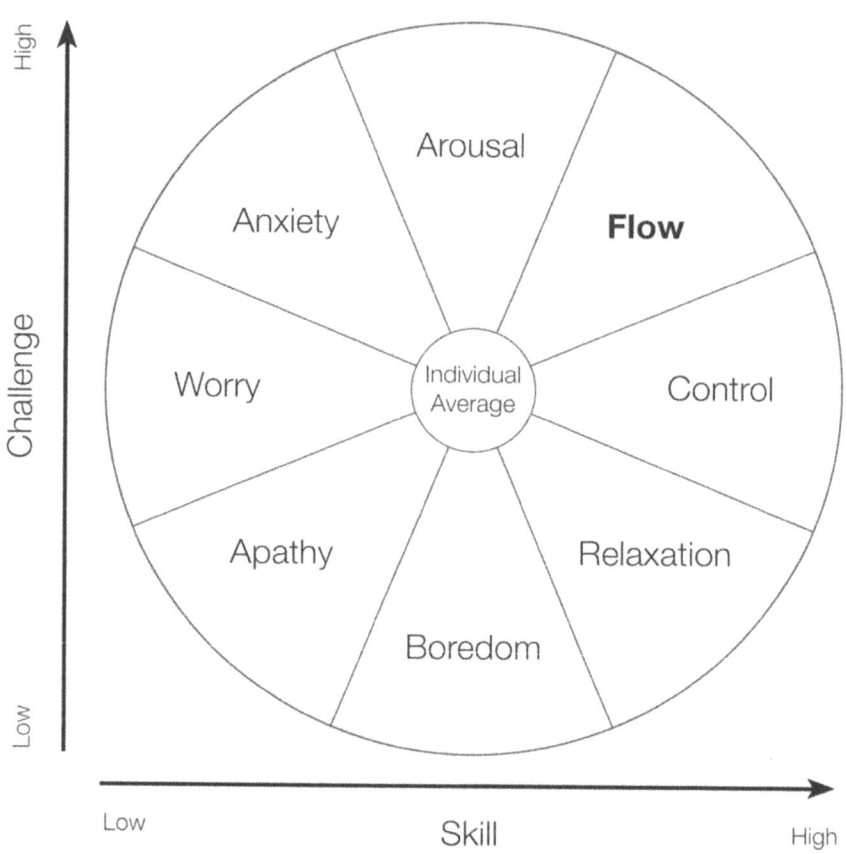

Figure 2: *Eight-Channel Model of Subjective Experience*
Figure by Susan A. Jackson (2024). Adapted by permission from Massimini and Carli (1988), p.270.[5]

Moving further left in the model, we find that all too familiar experience when we feel out of our depth: *Anxiety*. In addition to physiological increases in arousal, we are concerned about what we can do in this high-challenge situation and have doubts about our ability to be successful. Lowering the challenge to a moderate level can ease the strong emotions that accompany anxiety, but because we continue to perceive our skill level to be low, we are still concerned about what may happen and *Worry*, the next experience in this model, results.

The way out of anxiety or worry? One option (not recommended) is to drop the challenges completely down, to be at the same low level as our perceived skills. The resultant experience is perhaps the most negative of all in this model, a state called *Apathy*. We have no motivation, as there is nothing to aim for, and we can't be bothered to take action in any case. Apathy is a dangerous place to stay for long and can lead to depression if one does not move out of it by either developing new skills, finding new challenges, or extending both skills and challenges.

Antonella Delle Fave shared that in her laboratory's extensive cross-cultural research on the different experiences defined by the relative ratio of challenges and skills, one psychological state always came out as the most negative to be in. This is the low-challenge, low-skill experience termed apathy. While people don't enjoy apathy, flow research indicates it is a state regularly experienced by many.

Another regular and mostly negative state to experience is *Boredom*, an experience where challenge and skill remain low, but not zero as in apathy. In boredom, our skills are much higher than the challenges available to us—and this is what eventually leads to that state of being bored with the situation we are in. Boredom is not enjoyable, and skill is required to move out of this state. Antonella and I talked about how in the times that we grew up in, boredom was perceived as a springboard for inventing new things to do. Or if this was not possible, we tolerated boredom. This is itself a skill and one that today's young people may not easily develop. With so much at one's fingertips in our technologically-driven age, young people often have a low tolerance for boredom. The risk is that boredom becomes easily intolerable and, from there, can slip into being experienced as pathological. Initial acceptance of the feeling of boredom can, coupled with knowledge of flow, allow one to create a personal challenge that leads one out of this state. By finding a new goal in the middle of an otherwise boring situation and bringing one's attention to the chosen direction, a setting that one cannot wait to get out of can morph into an absorbing experience.

Continuing with the eight-channel experience model, we move from boredom to relaxation by continuing to develop skills while at the same time finding small challenges to direct our attention toward. When in the state of relaxation, we are enjoying our ability to demonstrate skills in a relatively low-challenge situation. For high performers, finding activities that are relaxing provides much-needed recovery time from the usual peak demands of their work/performance setting.

A different way to manage anxiety and worry other than lowering the challenge level of a situation (which involves moving into boredom/apathy) is to learn to be okay with the uncomfortable feelings worry and anxiety bring. That is the focus of the next chapter. Knowing that one of the subjective experiences in the eight-channel model is arousal—and that arousal is a more neutral state than worry or anxiety to be in—moving clockwise from worry and anxiety to arousal shifts one's experience in a positive manner. It also puts one closer to flow state, which, as Figure 2 shows, is adjacent to arousal in the model.

Making the Model Practical

I find this eight-channel model of subjective experience provides a nice visual way to understand the different experiences we may have in the performance settings in which we operate. When working with clients, I sometimes ask them to mark an X on the model to denote their primary experience in a performance, event, or workday that we are reviewing in a session. This exercise can be developed from a one-off assessment to track experience across the length of a performance, event, or period of time at work. Charting the movement from one channel to another can help a client understand the factors influencing their quality of experience as they take part in different tasks and challenges in their performance setting. Below is a self-assessment you can do to assess your own experience using this eight-channel model.

Self-assessment of Subjective Experience

In the model below, reflect on your experience today. Mark on the model with an X the experiences you've had as you've gone through your day, and write next to each X what you were doing at the time. You might also like to complete this exercise when you engage in your main performance/activity (you might like to photocopy the self-reflection figure below and use it over time) to develop self-awareness of your experience when performing. Finally, mark with an * the channel/s of experience you aim to be in when taking part in your main performance setting.

A key learning from these models of subjective experience is the importance of recognizing how challenges and skills stack up for you in the situations that matter to you. The models clearly demonstrate how we can experience things quite differently through changes in the relative balance of challenges and skills. It is important to remember that these models work on the movement of challenges and skills from average levels of both qualities, remembering that this average level is specific to each individual. Thus, the first and arguably most important pre-condition for flow is met when you move beyond your own average level of both skill and challenge in your activity of interest. Movement toward the flow channel may take you through the route of relaxation and control or via the less tolerable route of worry, anxiety, and to arousal. Whichever direction you take, movement toward the top right of the models is helping you to find flow.

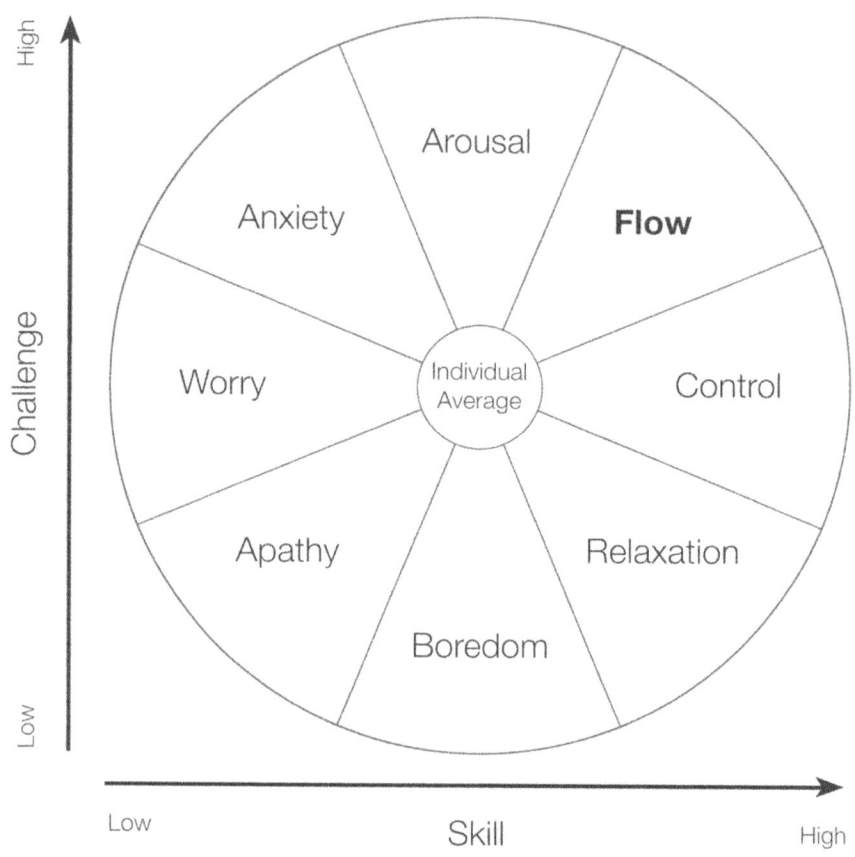

Subjective Experience Self-Reflection Exercise
© Susan A. Jackson, 2024

Self-Reflection Exercise:

1. Where have you been today? Mark on the model with an X the primary experiences you've had and write next to the X what you were doing at the time.
2. Where do you want to be when doing an important task or activity? Mark with a * (or a series of *** across channels) where you aim to be when taking part in your main performance setting.

It's Perceptions of Challenges and Skills That Matter

There's another critically important thing to remember about the challenges and skills equations. The models of flow I've outlined here are psychological models. This means that what matters more than the objective level of challenges and skills in any situation is the individual's *perception* of the challenges and of their skills. While challenges often tend to be viewed somewhat objectively, as they reside outside of the individual, perception of skills can vary dramatically between individuals of an equal ability level, as well as for the one individual at different times. One can be very highly skilled but lack confidence in certain situations. I saw this all too clearly when interviewing World and Olympic champions about their experiences in their sport. While at first a bit surprised to hear athletes at the very top of their sport referring to wavering confidence, over time, I came to understand that confidence can be unsteady for many high-level athletes despite all the evidence supporting their outstanding skill levels. I've since seen this lack of stability in confidence arising with many high-performing individuals in my psychology consulting. Developing confidence and trust in one's skills is an area I frequently explore with clients, be they elite athletes, high-performing executives, medical doctors training for their specialty exams, or individuals pursuing personal improvement in particular areas of their lives.

Some individuals have learned to trust themselves, regardless of the stakes of the high-pressure situation they are in. These athletes can be trusted to take the game-winning shot. Michael Jordan is a classic example of an athlete who trusted in their skills consistently. We saw that on the court and in what Jordan said about thriving in high-pressure situations. I like this quote from MJ about trust:

> *You must expect great things of yourself before you can do them.*[6]

Jordan shows in this quote a perspective that many athletes struggle with—having trust in one's skills before these skills are fully realized. Many in high-performance situations wouldn't choose to take on a challenge that they've yet to demonstrate a skill set to match. No doubt the expectations and pressure to perform successfully drive this attitude, particularly where competition is involved. In the upcoming chapter on mastery mindset, a pathway to developing an openness to taking on high challenge and redefining success in one's own terms is described, providing an alternative perspective to consider.

Go a Little Bit Out of Your Depth

When listening to an early years' interview of the late David Bowie, one of the most influential musicians of the 20th century, I heard him beautifully describe this idea of being prepared to take on high challenge in order to produce one's best work:

> *If you feel safe in the area you're working in, you're not working in the right area. Always go a little further into the water than you feel you're capable of being in. Go a little bit out of your depth. And when you don't feel that your feet are quite touching the bottom, you're just about in the right place to do something exciting.*[7]

Bowie clearly understood from his own experiences the pathway to finding flow. If you remember one thing from this chapter on the models of flow, remember what Bowie said about going a little bit out of your depth and perceiving that experience of your feet not quite touching the ground as being exciting. That place where challenges and skills are both high, with the challenge taking you just a little out of your depth, opens up the opportunity for great things to occur through flow.

An athlete who lives life by this Bowie quote is outdoor rock climber Hazel Findlay. Hazel is one of the most skilled female climbers in the world. She has been rock climbing since she was four years old, thanks to her father, who introduced her to his own passion for climbing when she was at a young age. As a young climber, Hazel was a six-time junior British champion in indoor rock climbing. However, it was outdoor climbing that Hazel was most passionate about. Since she was 18, Hazel has been climbing challenging outdoor routes all over the world.

Hazel was the first British woman to climb E9, 8c free climb El Capitan, which she has repeated several times. She has put up first ascents all over the world. In 2022, she accompanied Alex Honnold, the legend of the Oscar-winning documentary *Free Solo*, on a climbing expedition to Greenland. Alex Honnold demonstrated in *Free Solo* an appetite for pushing the boundaries of challenge in climbing one of the largest and steepest rock faces in the world—without ropes. In a striking depiction of how one can define even an objectively extreme challenge through the lens of one's perceptions, Alex described his approach to climbing walls, including El Cap, without any protection as one of separating risk from consequence.

> *I like to differentiate between risk and consequence . . . .when I'm doing these hard free solos, I like to think that the risk, you know, the chance of me falling off, is quite low, even though the consequence is extremely high.*[8]

The Greenland trip that Hazel accompanied Alex on (and which did involve the use of ropes), is the subject of another National Geographic documentary, with the team on this expedition also collecting data to inform climate-change scientists. Led by glaciologist Dr. Heidi Sevestre, the scientific part of the team was investigating the impact of climate change on the glaciers, ice caps, and fjords in this remote part of the Artic.[9]

The documentary, called *Arctic Ascent*, provides a close-up insight into the challenges world-best climbers faced on this expedition. Hazel, Alex, and the team made two first ascents on very difficult walls in harsh conditions—snow, rain, crumbly rock, freezing temperatures, and/or strong winds! Along the way, they collected rock samples, and drilled temperature sensors into the wall, helping future scientists to monitor temperature change here in this remote part of the world.

Climbing on this expedition turned into a hugely challenging encounter for the entire expedition team. When first viewing the sea cliff wall known as Ingmikortilaq, Alex and Hazel were taken aback at the sheer size of this sea cliff; the 4000-foot wall is 1000 feet higher than El Capitan, made famous with Honnold's free solo climb up El Cap. It had never been climbed, and the nature of the rock wall and the sheer height of it, stretching straight upwards from the sea, meant that there was a high level of uncertainty about whether Ingmikortilaq could, in fact, be ascended or not. This understandably led to high levels of arousal in what was a very highly skilled team. Hazel described it thus:

> *You're in the middle of Greenland, with icebergs cracking beneath you and rocks falling down next to you, and if you fall, you're probably gonna die—your arousal level is going to be higher than if you're just like in the climbing gym.*

When they finally made the summit, Alex and Hazel described how they'd encountered fear many times through the ascent. Hazel shared with Alex at the summit how they'd come up a terrifying wall. Alex, not known for experiencing fear in the way most humans do, said that neither of them had climbed anything *"so consistently scary."* He remarked that it's the kind of climb that you do only if it matters enough to you. Having successfully made the first ascent on Ingmikortilaq, their joy was obvious. Returning to David Bowie and the idea of going out of your depth, Hazel and Alex had ventured to the edges of challenge, and afterward, they recognized that they'd done something really exciting while also contributing to understanding climate change.

In our interview, Hazel shared how important the challenge-skill balance is to her experience, to whether she finds flow.

> *The challenge and how I respond to the challenge is for me the biggest determining factor for whether I access flow or not.*

In addition to being a seriously good professional climber, Hazel is a climbing coach and a mental skills coach. She is also the founder of *Strong Mind* and hosts a podcast by this name. Hazel has one of the strongest minds in the climbing world. When I was discussing the climb up Ingmikortilaq, referencing the David Bowie quote about going a bit out of your depth, Hazel responded that during this climb, she was mostly "in deep water." She shared with me that for much of her Ingmikortilaq ascent, the challenge-skill balance was tipped in the direction of arousal and anxiety. However, Hazel recounted that she was able to find flow during parts of the climb and attributed this to her psychological skill set, plus the positivity and high confidence of her climbing partner, Honnold. The skills that Hazel drew on to allow her to not be freaked out during this climb that she described as terrifying included deep breathing, focusing on each move, not weighing herself down cognitively with doubts about what's coming next, and reminding herself that the climb was within her sphere of ability. She also made the most of the times she was not lead climbing to bring her high arousal level down. Through applying these psychological skills, Hazel was able to shift her experience from the anxiety channel toward the flow channel.

Another factor that helped Hazel to find flow on the Ingmikortilaq climb was the high level of motivation to achieve something of immense personal significance to her. When we have a strong why, it is possible to harness this motivation to help tip the scales back toward flow when they're gravitating toward anxiety.

> *Climbing a wall like that is just once in a lifetime. You never get that chance again to have that experience. And it's such a unique, memorable, amazing experience.*

I had the good fortune to meet Hazel through my work with the Australian-based Flow Centre, where she was part of the first cohort to complete training to become a Flow Coach. Hazel understands flow both conceptually and experientially. She was thus an excellent choice to be a case example for this book. Throughout the rest of *Experiencing Flow*, I interweave excerpts from an interview I conducted with Hazel on the topics at the core of this book. Hearing from a high-performing individual who is very familiar with flow and mindfulness gives us an opportunity to connect with the flow experience through the lens of someone who pushes their own personal boundaries and is open to their experience. Someone who's been prepared, to paraphrase Bowie, to have their "feet not quite touching the ground."

Balancing Challenges and Skills: Self-Reflection Exercise

To know which subjective experiences you're more likely to find yourself having when you engage in your main activity/performance setting, consider the following questions about your relative mix of perceived challenges and skills.

Challenge-Skill Balance Self-Reflection Questions

Do you have the right mix of Challenges (C) and Skills (S), i.e., your CS Balance, in your main performance setting?

What could you do with your CS Balance to help make your experience more flow-facilitative?

Can you set 2-3 goals for optimizing your CS Balance for the coming month?

What sources of feedback (internal and external) can you seek out, to know if you're on track for finding the CS Balance that primes you for flow?

CHAPTER 5

Moving From Anxiety to Flow via Acceptance

Anxiety Gets to Most of Us at Least Some of the Time

Anxiety is a common experience. Most people will feel anxious when confronted with challenges they are uncertain they can meet or simply when faced with life's general uncertainties. While anxiety is grounded in our body's natural response to stressful, uncertain, and downright scary situations, I've come to learn that our minds can have as much to do with the anxiety we experience as any associated increased physiological arousal response.

I've experienced anxiety throughout my life and have seen both its beneficial and its detrimental effects. When in situations of high challenge in performance arenas, anxiety has usually helped me harness additional energy and channel it into focus. However, there have certainly been times when anxiety during performance has prevented me from achieving what I might otherwise have been able to.

My personal interest in understanding anxiety has led me to explore different approaches to its management. I find the flow model of immense benefit when I am in challenging situations, as I recognize that when anxiety surfaces, flow is potentially not that far away, as described in Chapter 4 on the flow models. Learning to re-perceive the uncomfortable feelings of uncertainty and self-doubt as a potential opportunity to do something exciting casts anxiety in a whole new light.

Hazel described how perceptions of anxiety can influence our experience. Referring to a positive stress experience, known as eustress, Hazel explains how an openness to learning when experiencing stress can open the door to flow:

> *If we're able to learn when in eustress, we're able to have flow experiences. A key indicator in the climbing setting, and especially in terms of fear management, is that after a eustress experience, you feel like you want to do that thing again. You might need a rest. It might be, "I'll come back tomorrow," but you feel motivated, as you've experienced flow after feeling stress.*

Hazel describes how getting the challenge level right is critical when anxiety heightens:

> *It's more important for me to get the challenge level right when I have anxiety. I'm always thinking about the challenge-skill balance and finding the right challenge. But when I have anxiety, it's even more important for me. I'm going to be more cautious, and probably going to have to start at a much lower challenge level and increase it more incrementally than I might do on like a day when I feel really confident.*

Hazel went on to describe how, when anxious, she pays special attention to the psychological challenge level of climbing. She asks herself questions that target where anxiety is likely to surface: How much gear is on the climb? Is it in an exposed, wild place? Who are you climbing with? Do you really trust your belay partner?

I asked Hazel how frequently climbers experience anxiety. Her comments are certainly applicable for people who experience anxiety in settings outside of climbing, particularly where fear is involved:

> *It's pretty massive. I think it's probably the main thing that affects climbers' performance. I mean, climbing is a very psychologically demanding sport. It's just kind of ingrained within us to find climbing as a kind of naturally fearful thing. People don't think about that, and then they go, "Why am I so scared? This doesn't make sense rationally. I know I shouldn't be scared." So, they're constantly invalidating their experience. A lot of my job is actually getting people to connect with what their bodies are saying and to work with anxiety; rather than ignoring it, pushing it aside.*

Hazel refers to how trying to rationalize one's way out of anxiety leads to invalidating one's experience. It does little to reduce anxiety, instead causing an internal dialogue that takes one away from the actual experience, and it doesn't actually address the anxiety. A more effective approach is to work with the anxiety, developing skills and strategies that can be implemented when anxiety surfaces.

Mindfulness practices, which I describe in the coming chapters, have been very helpful to Hazel's and my own work, quieting an over-active mind and channeling attention into the present. I am so grateful to have developed a practice of meditation through taking up yoga over 30 years ago. Over the years, my physical practice of yoga has decreased due to injuries sustained in a lifetime of fairly intense sport involvement. However, as my yoga practice started to decrease, I began reading more and more about mindfulness as a western, evidence-based practice. The growth of interest in mindfulness in western society has developed in parallel with the fast-paced and technologically-focused world we live in. It's one that shows little sign of slowing down in its demands, nor the associated heightened stress it produces in many people.

While becoming informed about mindfulness through my own reading and professional development courses, I came across a psychological approach that has mindfulness skills as one of its key processes. I've found this approach very helpful for managing my own and my clients' anxiety. Acceptance and Commitment Therapy/Training (ACT for short) is a third-wave cognitive-behavioral approach to helping us navigate life. More than just navigating it, ACT helps us to live a satisfying, meaningful life, including finding flow. This is achievable from an ACT perspective through developing psychological skills to better manage our thoughts and feelings and by becoming clear on our values, which are then developed into actionable strategies that take us in the direction of what we want. The acronym ACT is pronounced 'act' to emphasize the skills and action-focused approach of the model. All of the ACT strategies help bring our attention to the present moment, a key pre-requisite for flow to occur.

Learning a Different Way to Relate to Anxiety through ACT

ACT was developed by Professor Steve Hayes in the 1980s. Hayes and colleagues developed a model that describes six psychological processes, which together help us to live with a level of psychological flexibility that is the ultimate goal of ACT. Psychological flexibility is defined as:

> *. . . the ability to contact the present moment more fully as a conscious human being and to change or persist in behavior when doing so serves valued ends. Psychological flexibility is established through six core ACT processes. Each of these areas is conceptualized as a positive psychological skill, not merely a method of avoiding psychopathology.*[1]

The six ACT process skills are acceptance, defusion from unhelpful thoughts, being in the present, observing one's experience, being clear on one's values, and taking goal-directed action toward one's identified values. In this chapter, I am going to pay particular attention to acceptance, as this is a powerful tool to help manage anxiety.

Hayes brought to his foundational work in developing ACT a background in cognitive-behavioral therapy and a strong personal experience of anxiety. I've heard Hayes speak about his direct experience with anxiety, which took him into panic disorders, first in public and then in the safety of his own home. He has described how, upon finding himself close to breaking point with unremitting anxiety and panic, he decided to try facing his strong emotions rather than his previous go-to of running away from them. This was the impetus to Hayes developing what we now know as the psychological approach of ACT. The essential first step that helped Hayes reduce the power anxiety and worry held over him was realizing that it was the struggle, as much as the difficult memory or feeling, that was amplifying negative experiences to fear or panic.

If you'd like to hear Hayes share his experience of anxiety and how it finally led him to find a new perspective to manage his troubling thoughts and feelings, you can watch his TEDx talk at the University of Nevada.[2]

"Never again will I run from me" is what Steve Hayes said to himself after his worst, and presumably last, panic attack. This new perspective on being with his experience led him to develop, along with a team of valued collaborators, the scientific model foundational to ACT. Notable early contributors to this development were Drs. Kelly Wilson and Kirk Strosahl, who are regarded as co-founders of ACT with Steve Hayes. The three together wrote the landmark book on ACT, titled *Acceptance and Commitment Therapy: The Process and Practice of Mindful Change*.

Hayes and colleagues recommended that anxiety and other difficult emotions can be understood and their intensity lessened through bringing acceptance to them. The word acceptance can mean different things. In ACT, it is accepting what is happening in the present moment. It does not necessarily mean you agree with, want, or condone what is happening. However, you do give up the struggle with the difficult emotions. In other words, you stop fighting with reality and instead open up to understanding what the experience is. By so doing, some of the power and intensity of the strong emotion, or unhelpful thought patterns, is defused. As with all ACT processes, acceptance is a learnable skill. With practice, one gets better at making room for difficult feelings and not being carried away by them.

In his TEDx, Hayes described that he came to ACT from recognizing that turning toward pain and suffering is turning toward meaning and purpose. Fellow ACT theorists have similarly described opening up to their life's difficulties as turning points for them. While attending an international ACT conference in Sydney in 2013, I had the opportunity to hear Steve Hayes speak, and to meet him. I found him to be a very dynamic and engaging presence.

Live it to Learn It

At the same conference in Sydney, I also attended a workshop by ACT co-founder Kelly Wilson. Kelly was like no other presenter I've met. He brought to the delivery of his workshop a rawness and intensity of feeling that engendered emotional responses in workshop attendees. Kelly seemed to teach by the principle, "live it to learn it." And Kelly had certainly lived it.

I remember interviewing Kelly during the conference on the lawn of the university campus where the event was being held. I was a writer and editor of a national yoga magazine at the time. I knew Kelly had taken up yoga with a passion, and I wanted to talk with him about how yoga fit into his thoughts on and experience with life from an ACT perspective.

Kelly came to yoga at age 54 and from a background of being, in his words, a lifelong committed non-exerciser. Through yoga, Kelly came into a dramatically different relationship with his body and with how he lived his life. I asked Kelly what brought him to yoga:

> *I was teaching a mindfulness exercise at a mindfulness retreat in 2009, an exercise involving inclining one's heart in the direction of different values. The exercise involves thinking of someone who you love without reservation. Then, imagine you were someone you loved like that—what would you do? While teaching the exercise, I asked myself, would I treat someone I love with the kind of casual disregard I treat myself? I came home and signed up at a local yoga studio for a year. I thought I wouldn't like it, but just as you take a sick child to a doctor, you do it anyway. But I fell in love with yoga.*

When I asked Kelly why he chose yoga, he told me that he remembered the mindfulness scholar, Jon Kabat-Zinn, having referred to yoga as 360-degree mindfulness. So, Kelly chose yoga as his mindfulness practice. He became immersed in yoga, finding what he described as a "kindness" in the practice. Kelly shared how learning to look after his body, cultivated through yoga, was a revelation to him. Having left home at 16 with the goal of hitchhiking around the US, he shared with me how things went dark very quickly.

> *By the time I was 17 years old, I was injecting drugs, and that was anything and everything. I was hanging out with drugstore cowboys—people who were robbing drugstores and trafficking in drugs. I was involved in that life from the time I moved out of my parent's house when I was 16 and until I was 30 years old. I was high every single day, except for a*

> *couple times when I got thrown in jail for a few days or put in the hospital. Even when I was in the hospital, I would get my friends to bring narcotics in to me. So, that was up until 1985. So, when I say I think human bodies are robust, at least mine is because it survived a lot of those experiences—some really harsh, like two packs of cigarettes a day, and gross intoxication every single day. Then, in 1985, I let go of all that stuff.*

Letting go was no easy process for Kelly. He decided he wanted to live, explaining that he had seen many of the guys he ran with die. And he decided to give up what he described as a fight with life. He was applying what he would later know as a key ACT psychological process, acceptance. Kelly described how this unfolded for him as he reached age 30:

> *Well, it was because I couldn't fight anymore. I couldn't. There had been, for a long time, a solace in getting high. As I got to 30, there was just nothing left, no solace left. There was just no place else to hide. I just couldn't get and stay high enough. My world had come apart again. I was empty. I had the good fortune of being put in a locked psychiatric hospital.*

Being inside a locked psychiatric hospital is not what most people would consider a preferred life situation. For Kelly, it saved his life and turned it around through discussions with people inside who introduced Kelly to acceptance and focusing on the next right thing to do. These insightful people probably had no idea how life-changing that would be for Kelly and for the many people his work in ACT has helped in subsequent years.

Somebody asked me in an interview the other day about my definition of success. I said, well, it's changed over time. In '85, I would have traded my life for one day when I didn't want to die. If you say that out loud, they'll put you in a hospital, and they did. When they put me in a locked psychiatric hospital, it was, fortunately, before the big pharma boom. 1985—Prozac doesn't come until 1987. There were some doctors, even then, because there were other anti-depressants and things, who looked to give me medication. But fortunately, there were enough people on the treatment team who pointed out, 'This guy has been putting drugs in his body for the last 15 years, every day. Let's let all the drugs be gone and then see what's left.' It took a couple of weeks to detox me, and then I had the good fortune to meet some people who taught me about acceptance and doing the next right thing, even when it didn't make any sense. I was able to get sober. I've been sober, off drugs and alcohol, since June 1, 1985.

Kelly Wilson is a dramatic example of turning one's life around 180 degrees. From having lived life on the edge of death as a young person to becoming a world-leading academic scholar and co-founder of ACT after deciding he did want to live and live meaningfully. From my experience with Kelly, I could see that he didn't just study and teach ACT—he lived it.

Hazel Findlay uses the principle of acceptance very successfully in helping climbers transform anxiety and fear so they can experience flow. Hazel shared that avoiding acceptance of fear is one of the factors that can most profoundly impact someone's progress.

Sometimes, people just can't accept that something is really challenging for them, and they just want it to be different. They just want to turn it off. They want to turn off that fear. They want to just be able to do the thing that they see other people do, because physically, maybe they can. But psychologically, they don't have the resources yet, and this can really get in the way because it causes people to put the challenge level too high. Like, "I know physically I could do that, and like, I know that if I just removed my anxiety, I could do it." But I'm like, you can't just remove your anxiety! This is a process, and so bringing acceptance can be powerful, saying to oneself, "Well, I'm okay actually, as I am right now."

Hazel's description of accepting experience, including recognizing when something is very challenging and being OK with the feeling of fear, is consistent with an ACT mindset. The acceptance of fear and anxiety also frees up space mentally to allow focused attention on the task, which then may facilitate flow.

As the experiences of Steve Hayes and Kelly Wilson demonstrate, we can learn important lessons through people who provide us with clear examples of facing and accepting fear. Akshay Nananvati is another example of someone who has turned their life around by doing so. Akshay has learned through early drug addiction and then wartime and subsequent PTSD experiences that struggle is not something to escape but rather embrace because it leads to unparalleled growth. Akshay is a United States Marine veteran, speaker, entrepreneur, ultra-runner, and author. Fearvana[3] is the name of his organization, and one of its goals is to help people transform their relationship with fear, anxiety, and stress and to see these as catalysts for change and growth. Akshay's "great soul crossing," a planned solo crossing of Antarctica in November 2024, is an example of putting yourself fully on the line. People like Akshay, who play on the edges of human experience, teach us how to grow by facing our struggles head-on. In a podcast with performance psychologist Michael Gervais, Akshay shared his outlook on life and on finally feeling OK to step into the arena, where challenges and fears are faced:

> *The arena is where the wisdom lies. You have to go into the arena. That is where the wisdom is, the growth, the awakening, the bliss that is the human experience.*[4]

Becoming Psychologically Flexible

Akshay, Hazel, and ACT leaders Hayes and Wilson, are examples of individuals who have learned to step into the arena to fully live their lives. In doing so, they have accomplished great things and, on the journey, have learned to become psychologically flexible.

Developing flexibility psychologically is a key concept not just in ACT—it also influences the likelihood of experiencing flow. The overarching goal of the six processes of the ACT model, of which acceptance is one, is the attainment of psychological flexibility. Psychological flexibility is achieved when one can stay in the present moment, even when experiencing difficult thoughts, feelings, and sensations. The ACT approach resonates so strongly with me because it is about developing positive psychological skills. I've found through working with ACT in my own life, as well as teaching it to others, that I've learned to hold my thoughts and emotions a bit more lightly. Doing so has enabled me to stay more in the present moment and not get so tossed around by negative thoughts or unpleasant feelings.

From what we know about how flow occurs, the ACT approach can be considered a well-structured pathway to optimal experience. What I've learned from ACT is that once you bring yourself to the present moment, the next step is to focus on something that matters to you in what you are presently doing and working toward. By repeatedly taking actions that move you in the direction of what matters to you, life becomes richer and more meaningful. This behavior, plus the letting go of unhelpful thoughts and feelings, facilitates flow by helping you become fully present in your own life. As we have seen from people who have lived it, the ACT model also provides a framework from which to understand and manage anxiety. Rather than fight, ignore, or run from fear and anxiety, ACT provides what may first seem a counter-intuitive approach: to accept it. Both research and life experiences provide support for the proposition of turning *toward* the experience of anxiety. By bringing acceptance to anxiety, it is possible to defuse the intensity of it while at the same time moving toward what is most important in what one is doing at any given moment. In this way, ACT can be a useful pathway to move from the anxiety quadrant of experience and toward flow.

Identify your Anxiety Challenges

Self-Reflection Exercise: To help you understand how acceptance works as an anxiety mitigator, identify one area in your life where you experience more anxiety than you are comfortable with. Name this area, and jot down how anxiety shows up for you in this life domain (ask yourself: how do you know that you are anxious?). Make a goal that the next time you are in this situation, you will focus on bringing acceptance to your anxiety. It will help if you can identify a cue (simple cues are a stick-it-note in a visible place or a rubber band around your wrist) to remind you to bring acceptance when you're next in this anxiety-provoking situation.

CHAPTER 6

Moving From Boredom to Mastery and Flow

The problem human beings face is not that we aim too high and fail, but that we aim too low and succeed.

—*Michelangelo*

A Pathway Out of Boredom

In the last chapter, we looked at how we can shift out of the experience of anxiety and possibly into flow by developing our skills of being in the present moment and cultivating acceptance. In this chapter, we are going to look at the other side of the challenge-skill balance equation: when skills outweigh challenges. Here, we move into relaxation initially but soon into boredom if we remain at a fixed level of challenge while continuing to develop our skills.

Boredom is defined in the challenge-skill balance model as the condition we typically experience when skills significantly outweigh challenges. What usually happens when you are bored? Do you notice that a task that once involved some level of interest for you no longer has any attraction or enjoyment? Do you stick with the activity or look for an exit? Even if you can't make a physical exit, mentally, you're probably likely to check out. So, for example, in a job you find boring, you may show up because of some external force (e.g., money or the expectations of others). However, you may bring only minimal attention and effort to what you are doing, because you don't need a significant amount of either to meet your goal. Without investing our attention in what we are doing, we easily become bored. Conversely, by deciding to focus attention on something, we can become interested and engaged in what might have, at first perception, seemed like a boring activity. Mike described it like this:

> *If you are interested in something, you will focus on it, and if you focus attention on anything, it is likely that you will become interested in it. Many of the things we find interesting are not so by nature but because we took the trouble of paying attention to them.*[1]

In this quote, Mike demonstrates the critical role that paying attention has on our resultant quality of experience. Learning how to focus our attention better is one of the great gifts of mindfulness, detailed in Chapter 7. Setting personal goals is also important in situations where we might otherwise describe our experience as boring. Moving to the next level, from the goals we set to being aware of the motivational influences or orientations that precede these goals, can have an even more significant impact on our subjective experience. Because the area of motivational orientation is so important to quality of experience, this chapter will focus on two psychological approaches that explain how our orientations greatly influence the quality of our resultant experience. Adopting a mastery perspective influences our effort, engagement, and experience of either flow or boredom.

The two psychological approaches I am going to focus on to help us understand how to develop a mastery perspective are those of Carol Dweck and John Nicholls. Both approaches place emphasis on how we perceive our skills and how we develop belief in our potential in achievement situations. This is centrally important to the horizontal axis of the challenge-skill balance models that predict quality of experience, as described in Chapter 4. Perception of skills influences not only whether we feel anxious in a challenging situation but also whether we feel bored in a situation lacking challenge. With a mastery perspective, we perceive our skills as a malleable quality, something we can improve with an investment of effort and time. The adoption of a mastery perspective is, as we shall see through an overview of the theoretical approaches of Dweck and Nicholls, a pathway out of boredom. While Dweck and Nicholls use different language to describe their respective approaches to understanding motivation and achievement, I find the idea of a mastery perspective encompasses key principles from both approaches in relation to perceptions of skills and how skills can be developed. Remembering that the operational definition of flow is based on the relationship of challenges to skills, how we define our skills, and how we perceive we can develop these skills becomes critically important on the journey to finding flow.

Growth and Fixed Mindset

You've probably heard of growth mindset, made famous through the excellent research and writings of Carol Dweck. With the publication of *Mindset* in 2006, the argument for approaching life with a growth mindset over a fixed mindset began to take hold, especially in educational settings. Dweck summarized the differences between the two mindsets in an article in Harvard Business Review[2]: When you have a growth mindset you see ability and success as coming from such things as hard work, learning, and good strategies. Someone with a fixed mindset sees ability and success as fixed, or as Dweck refers to it, as "innate gifts." The problem with a fixed mindset is nicely described by Dweck in her 2016 revised edition of *Mindset:*

> *Believing that your qualities are carved in stone—the fixed mindset—creates an urgency to prove yourself over and over. If you have only a certain amount of intelligence, a certain personality, and a certain moral character—well, then you'd better prove that you have a healthy dose of them.*[3]

A growth mindset trumps a fixed mindset because it leads to higher achievement, mainly because, as Dweck describes it, *"You worry less about looking smart and put more energy into learning."*[4]

In her *Harvard Business Review* article, Dweck clarifies some misconceptions about growth mindset. She argues that we all are a mix of fixed and growth mindsets. It is not, as some would believe, an either-or proposition. Even if we see ourselves as being mostly motivated by learning and expanding our skills, there are likely to be some situations that trigger a fixed mindset. Dweck argues that it is important to identify our "fixed mindset triggers." Perhaps these might be a new challenge, being criticized, continually hitting dead ends, or performing worse than others in a public setting. The triggers are likely to be different across individuals. Learning to recognize and then manage your key fixed mindset triggers can help shift you back into a growth mindset. Whatever mindset you carry into a particular situation will influence your behavior, experience, and what you can achieve.

Another negative outcome of a fixed mindset is that it tends to keep us in our comfort zone. Climber Hazel Findlay described how this avoidance of challenge shrinks our risk zone:

> *If you remove all challenge and never expose yourself to challenging situations, you don't get the chance to grow and learn. And so, you lose resilience. I mean, that's how social anxiety can become worse and worse and worse because people slowly take away anything challenging from their lives.*
>
> *And that's what so many climbers do in relation to falling. They say, "Okay, well, falling is a scary part of climbing. I don't like it." They then avoid it. Someone can climb for 20, 30 years and never become more comfortable falling. Then they ask themselves,*

> *"Why am I not comfortable with this? I've climbed for so long."* To which I reply, *"You've climbed for a long time, but you've taken like two falls in your whole climbing life. Of course, you're not going to be comfortable with it!"*

Avoiding what causes us to feel worried, fearful, or anxious does not take away the fear. Rather, it takes away opportunities for learning, growth, and engagement while the propensity for being fearful remains. Shrinking our risk zone shrinks our life.

I had the good fortune to learn about growth and fixed mindset during my graduate studies. I took an achievement motivation class with Carol Dweck in 1987 when she was a professor of psychology at the University of Illinois (U of I) at Urbana-Champaign. As part of my Masters in sport psychology at the U of I, I had the opportunity to take several excellent courses in motivation through the psychology department. In Dweck's small group graduate course, our major assignment was to develop a research project to assess mastery and performance goals, the terminology Dweck was using at that time for what is now popularly known as growth and fixed mindset. As part of our project, we included Dweck's implicit theories of intelligence, which underlie mindset and have to do with how we perceive intelligence. A fixed mindset is associated with a belief that intelligence is a fixed and uncontrollable state: what Dweck referred to as an entity theory of intelligence. A growth mindset views intelligence as something that can be cultivated; it evolves incrementally in line with our efforts and learning strategies.

With a fixed mindset, success (like intelligence) is viewed as being based on innate ability or fixed traits. Basically, you have a certain amount of ability, and that's it. Therefore, the goal in achievement settings is to protect your perceptions of ability and to avoid looking "dumb." In contrast, with a growth mindset, success and abilities are based on hard work, training, and learning. Meaning we can all get better at something through working on it.

Effort is viewed very differently with fixed and growth mindsets, as Dweck explained:

> *In one world, effort is a bad thing. It, like failure, means you're not smart or talented. If you were, you wouldn't need effort. In the other world, effort is what makes you smart or talented.*[5]

One misconception about growth mindset that Dweck wrote about in a 2016 revision of *Mindset* is that it is *all* about effort. She pointed out that the process involves more than just effort. It is a combination of hard work, a willingness to try new strategies (especially when the strategies one has been using aren't working), and seeking input and feedback from others. Growth mindset is about development of ability or skills—the horizontal axis of the challenge-skill balance model of flow.

> *A growth mindset is about believing people can develop their abilities. It's that simple.*[6]

Understanding a Mastery Perspective through Task and Ego Orientations

At the same time as Dweck was developing her ideas about growth and fixed mindset, Nicholls was developing his own approach to understanding perceptions of ability, especially in children. Nicholls' work helps provide another perspective on how boredom can either arise or be circumvented. I got to experience firsthand an understanding of John Nicholls' work, as I had with Carol Dweck. In another research project at the U of I, this time in Professor Glyn Roberts' class on the social psychology of sport, we were given the task of interviewing a researcher whose work in the achievement motivation area was of interest to us. I traveled to nearby Purdue University to interview Professor John Nicholls, whose work on conceptions of ability, effort, and task difficulty I found very interesting. Nicholls emphasized the importance of conceptions of ability in his theory.[7] He argued that the goal of achievement behavior is competence, or demonstration of ability.

Competence, Nicholls argued, could be defined either in a differentiated or a less differentiated way. The differentiated conception he termed *ego involvement*, where ability is inferred from comparing performance and effort. Higher perceived effort infers lower ability. Or, put another way, if you have to try hard, that indicates low ability on a task. Nicholls further distinguished between ego-involved individuals with high or low perceived ability. High-perceived ability individuals were predicted to only put out high effort when it was perceived necessary for demonstrating high ability. They would avoid putting out effort on normatively easy or very difficult tasks, choosing to apply effort only on normatively moderately difficult tasks. This is because in very easy or very difficult tasks, to apply effort would demonstrate a lack of ability. Either because an easy task shouldn't take much effort to complete; or because if something was very difficult, one would risk not succeeding, and that would also demonstrate a lack of ability. If an individual started out with low perceived ability, the impact on effort was even worse. Effort would be low across most scenarios, and they would also be likely to have high anxiety and little motivation to engage. Such lack of engagement and avoidance of all challenge would lead to boredom and poor perceptions of self.

With a less differentiated conception of ability, which Nicholls referred to as *task involvement*, difficulty and ability judgments are self-referenced. The higher the effort needed for mastery, the higher the perceived ability. Performance is directly tied in with effort; the more effort, the more successful one was in a task.

In our interview, Nicholls emphasized the importance of language to understand the motivations of people who are ego-involved versus task-involved:

> *If you say someone wants to show they're smart—that language really only works for ego involvement. If you're consciously thinking about ability, then you're more likely to be in the ego-involved mode, and you're using this differentiated concept of ability. Whereas you can still get a sense of competence and accomplishment just from doing your best at something.*

Nicholls argued that as one progresses from childhood to adulthood, the implications of ego involvement become more striking:

> *Ego involvement is likely to be more debilitating the more this concept gets developed. You can still get it in young kids, but it's not so likely to mess you up when concepts around ability are less differentiated. When ability is capacity, not being smart is a rather more severe thing.*

While children can be ego-involved, Nicholls argued the implications were less than for adults because children still had the less differentiated concept of ability. Over time, particularly when reinforced by the environment one grows up in, some people will become strongly ego-oriented, and as Nicholls stated, perceiving oneself *not* to be smart carries with it strong consequences. As adults, we can choose to employ either a more or a less differentiated conception of ability. As well as developmental factors, Nicholls argued that personal disposition and situational factors would influence whether one chooses ego or task involvement.

Unfortunately, the work of John Nicholls was cut short by his untimely death in 1994 at age 54. The insightful work of Nicholls remains in journal articles and in a book he wrote called *The Competitive Ethos and Democratic Education*, published in 1989. In *The Competitive Ethos,*

Nicholls discusses how the strong emphasis on interpersonal competition in Western society leads to more ego involvement, and this means, for some, a negative and alienating educational experience.

John Nicholls' ideas resonated with me, and it was a special experience to visit and interview him. He had a strong interest in how young children interact with their environment, and the ways in which he described their absorption in tasks, mostly unconcerned with what others around them were doing, reminded me of the experience of flow. The unselfconscious involvement that we can observe in young children gives us a glimpse into what being in flow looks like.

I took the concepts of task and ego involvement and included them as variables in my flow research. I have consistently found that task involvement (or growth mindset in Dweck's language) is more strongly associated with flow than ego involvement. Athletes high in task involvement report experiencing flow more frequently than athletes low in task involvement. This relationship makes intuitive sense, with a motivation to develop mastery fostering the total concentration on a task that defines flow. And when one is motivated to develop mastery and to apply effort in learning and competitive situations, it is unlikely that boredom will be experienced. Conversely, when someone is ego involved (performance-oriented in Dweck's language), and when perceived ability is low, or when a task is considered to be easy or very difficult, the resultant low effort would lead to boredom. An understanding of how we are likely to apply effort in achievement settings helps us to recognize the precursors to boredom—and to its opposite, engagement. Engagement is the road to flow.

It wasn't surprising to hear Hazel say she doesn't get bored because she has become skilled at upping the challenge level when the conditions for boredom arise. Even if that means doing so somewhat artificially, as Hazel explains:

You can also kind of artificially tweak the challenge. For example, there may only be easy climbs at this crag. So, I challenge myself by doing a climb nine times in a row as quickly as possible. Or I may do a climb not using this hold or that hold.

The Problem with Chronic Boredom

Boredom is a very unsatisfying experience, and if left unchecked, it leads to the even more negative state of apathy. During apathetic states, there is no challenge and, therefore, no skills needed. Nothing can be produced in apathy, and more concerning is the deleterious effect apathy has on one's disposition. Depression can easily set in, along with a drop in physical health. Therefore, learning ways to avoid boredom is important to keep moving forward. Having clear goals that are tied to personally meaningful values will help keep boredom at bay. When one's life is focused on learning and effort, that is, a mastery perspective, the risk of boredom decreases, and clear, sustainable pathways to personal achievement are available. Mastery also provides the direction to experiencing flow, as Hazel describes:

My focus on mastery orientation allows a lot of the other potential distractions and barriers to flow and performance dissolve almost. It's like I go climbing. Someone does a climb before you, and you start to feel a bit like, "Oh, no, I don't really like that. I want to be able to do it." Little comparisons like that. Little ego-based things, basically. Or, like, I feel a bit shit because I didn't do this grade, or I haven't climbed anything hard for a while. You know, all of that kind of social, sticky ego mindset stuff kind of falls away when I can be solid in my focus on mastery. For me, climbing is about mastery, and I'm still on that path, and everything I do is part of that path. Coming back to that is really powerful.

Hazel illustrates well how the generally loud voice of the ego mind can be quieted by switching to a mastery perspective. Hazel and I concurred that flow can be the experiential result of focusing on personal mastery. Whereas with an ego mindset, you are likely to be less motivated to engage in the challenge that you need to engage in in order to grow and experience flow.

I'll finish this chapter with a quote by Albert Einstein, viewed as one of the most intelligent scientists of all time, demonstrating how important effort and persistence are to success.

> *It's not that I'm so smart; it's just that I stay with problems longer.*
>
> —*Albert Einstein*

CHAPTER 7

Finding a Pathway to Flow via Mindfulness

When I go to the climbing gym, pretty much every teenage lad in there is way stronger than me. But they can't climb what I climb, and obviously, the technical ability is massive, you know. It takes a long time to master the movement of climbing. But part of mastering the movement in the technique is also what you do with your attention. If you're busy being too stressed, you're too tense. If you're distracted, it is going to be much harder for you to learn movement skills. I've spent a lot of time focusing on that mental challenge of climbing.

—Hazel Findlay

Hazel is a very highly skilled climber and no doubt it is the combination of having focused for many years on developing both physical and psychological skills that has contributed to her accomplishments and to becoming a sought-after climbing coach. Hazel has placed particular importance on developing her mindfulness skills, as will be illustrated later in this chapter.

I focus in this chapter on sharing my own journey to mindfulness and how I came to understand that mindfulness is a foundationally important skill in finding flow. In the chapter to follow, I cover some important mindfulness skills and practices that you may wish to incorporate into your life journey.

Many years after first learning about flow and then spending many more years researching this optimal state, I became interested in mindfulness. Having completed graduate degrees in sport psychology, I was familiar with the suite of psychological skills that were promoted as being beneficial for peak performance—skills such as goal setting, intrinsic motivation, concentration, relaxation, and imagery. Mindfulness, however, was rarely mentioned during my years in grad school, which spanned the late 1980s to early 1990s. Today, mindfulness is more than a buzzword in psychology and society in general. Since the late 90s, there has been an exponential growth in research on mindfulness, plus awareness of the benefits of mindfulness across society.

A key person behind the development of mindfulness in the West has been Jon Kabat-Zinn, who found that he was able to make breakthrough progress with chronic pain patients in his work at the Massachusetts Medical School by teaching mindfulness skills to these individuals. Kabat-Zinn had spent years immersing himself in Zen Buddhist meditation and hatha yoga traditions. Finding much wisdom in these areas, he brought them into his clinical work, and went on to develop mainstream western science-based mindfulness programs and practices.

I came to mindfulness through the practice of yoga. While I began yoga for the physical practice, I stayed for the meditation.

Learning About Mindfulness

My favorite part of the yoga class was the final relaxation, often called yoga nidra, where we could lie still and focus on our breathing and on relaxing the physical body. Having been involved in speed and power sports for most of my life, lying still was not something I was accustomed to, other than when asleep. Here on the yoga mat, I found myself going into something resembling sleep, yet it was also a state of heightened awareness.

Knowing the best way to learn something is to teach it, I undertook yoga teacher training. Here, I learned about how breathing and meditation practices are integral to the overall practice of yoga. Through learning about the ancient teachings behind yoga, I came to appreciate how much yoga is, at its essence, a practice for the mind. The earliest known writings about yoga are Patanjali's yoga sutras, written over 1500 years ago. In the sutras, Patanjali sets out a sequence of eight steps that comprise yoga, and only one of these involves the physical postures, called asana,[1] which are often incorrectly perceived to be the purpose of yoga. Asana translated means sitting postures, and the purpose of asana was to prepare the body to sit for long periods of time comfortably, in order to engage in meditation and stillness. So, becoming flexible and strong through physical practices in yoga was to facilitate one being able to be still for long periods of time in meditation. This is quite different from how yoga has often been promoted in the West, focusing almost exclusively on the physical practice of asana. This was neither how nor why yoga was developed.

Right at the start of his Yoga Sutras, Patanjali set out that the purpose of yoga is to calm the fluctuations of the mind. This second sutra is translated from the ancient Sanskrit as "Yoga is the stilling of movement in the mind."[2]

Learning about the essential purpose of yoga through these ancient writings was very important for me. The parts of a yoga class that I was instinctively drawn toward—breathing and meditation components—were seen by the ancient yogis as the primary reason for engaging in a yoga practice.

My classes started to develop more of a focus on meditation, and the wonderful relaxation practice of yoga nidra. Then, I started to teach stand-alone meditation/relaxation classes and workshops. And over time, my "yoga" classes became less frequent, and I focused in on developing the discipline of mindfulness through the practice of meditation.

As I delved deeper into mindfulness, I started listening to audiobooks, podcasts, and interviews with leading meditation teachers, as well as taking teacher training courses in the area. Thus began my learning about Western mindfulness and the ever-growing body of research on its benefits. This growth in popularity of mindfulness came about in large part due to the efforts of leading mindfulness practitioners who had visited the East, dived deep into yogic and meditative practices, and brought their learnings back with them to the West. Some were psychologists, such as Jack Kornfield and Tara Brach. Others were meditation seekers whose own journeys led them to share their wisdom by founding meditation centers, such as Joseph Goldstein and Sharon Salzberg. Central to the exponential growth of mindfulness in the West was the foundational work of Jon Kabat-Zinn. It is Kabat-Zinn's clear and accessible definition of mindfulness that inspired and guided many teachers, myself included:

> *Mindfulness is paying attention in a particular way: on purpose, in the present moment, and non-judgmentally.*[3]

This widely used definition of mindfulness demonstrates how mindfulness and flow are linked—they both center around how one pays attention. Being mindful is having purposeful, present-focused attention. Becoming skilled in mindfulness can open the door to the complete and often effortless attention that defines flow.

A variation to Jon Kabat-Zinn's definition of mindfulness has been proposed by researchers Brown and Ryan, who describe mindfulness as *"open or receptive attention to and awareness of ongoing events and experiences."*[4] This definition reinforces the notion of becoming absorbed in the present when in a mindful state. It also emphasizes, as does the definition by Jon Kabat-Zinn, that attention is on present events and experiences—not our ongoing mind chatter. By bringing attention to what is actually happening around us, rather than what our minds tell us is happening, we unlock a door to flow. How mindfulness is particularly relevant to flow will be explored in the next section.

Mindfulness, Self-Awareness, and Flow

I asked Hazel Findlay how important mindfulness was to her performance and work:

> *It's very important for sure. I use it as a tool before and mid performance a lot. It's a way for me to be able to access presence more easily, and that helps me with almost everything I do in life. It helps me not to be wrapped up with thoughts and emotions in a way that's not serving me. It creates some space and distance between thoughts and emotions. I'm less reactive. I can be more accepting of the present moment and more grateful for it as well.*

I like the way Hazel describes mindfulness as allowing her to access presence more easily. This is essentially what mindfulness is—accessing the present moment. I asked Hazel whether developing a practice in mindfulness and meditation led to any change in her experience in climbing, including her frequency of flow experience. Hazel shared that it was easier to get into flow through having developed skills in mindfulness:

> *The main thing is that I'm more self-aware. Whereas before, I would have been lost in thought. Agitated, but not really knowing why I was agitated. I wouldn't know how to change or modify my experience. Now, through mindfulness, I'm more self-aware. I notice these things, and I can change and modify things. And this creates a pathway to flow.*

Here, Hazel highlights an important skill that is developed through mindfulness—the skill of self-awareness. No longer at the mercy of her thoughts and feelings, Hazel learned to notice what was happening in her experience and to make appropriate adjustments. The end result?

A pathway to flow was found—something I realized for myself when delving into mindfulness practice and teaching.

Mindfulness is relevant to experiencing flow, and flow is relevant to understanding mindfulness. Through my journey to mindfulness, I came to see how this skill and way of being can provide a pathway to flow. Mindfulness practices help us to develop greater awareness—of where our mind is and what it is like for our mind to be in the present moment. Flow only occurs in the present moment. When we are in performance situations, we may have learned and/or have been encouraged to focus on outcomes, such as how well we are doing in relation to others or what the stats tell us about how well we performed. This is OK when it occurs *after* you've finished your performance but is generally not helpful *during* performance. As discussed in the chapter on growth mindset and flow, how we perceive achievement and success can be based on comparisons with others or with our own previous past performances and efforts. The latter will be more helpful to our confidence and more likely to allow us to focus on the present during performance. Doing so will increase the chances of experiencing flow. Through the practice of mindfulness, we can improve our ability to focus on the present. Hence, we improve our flow readiness.

While mindfulness can facilitate flow, and while mindfulness shares some common characteristics with flow, it is not the same as flow. Both involve a present-moment focus and suspension of judgments from the self-critical mind. Mindfulness does not require the high-challenge, high-skill equation that operationally defines flow. Nor does it necessarily involve all the dimensions of flow detailed in Chapter 3. The definitions of mindfulness provided above indicate the way in which mindfulness facilitates flow—by bringing attention to the present moment in a non-judgmental way, and in a way that keeps you aware of your ongoing experience. Once flow is attained, one is in a state of total absorption, and there's no longer the need, as generally occurs in mindfulness, to apply effort to keep bringing attention back to the present moment and out of one's thoughts. Developing skills in mindfulness is an excellent way to make flow experiences more likely to occur; hence the focus on exploring mindfulness in this and the next chapter.

When we are focused in the present, our experience tends to be more enjoyable, and we perform the tasks in front of us better. The growth of mindfulness throughout many sectors of Western society over the last 25 years has been considerable. This growth in popularity of mindfulness has occurred as society has become increasingly fast-paced and technologically driven. While we can do more through technology, we are often expected to *constantly* be doing so, creating pressure. Plus, there is an expectation that we will juggle several things at once—leading to a distracted mind and, often, a stressful experience. Mindfulness provides a path to stillness in the mind, an experience that might otherwise be absent from our lives.

As awareness of mindfulness has grown, the benefits experienced through the practice have led to its uptake in many domains. A cover story by *TIME* in February 2014 on mindfulness is a testament to how mainstream the practice had become by the early 2000s.[5] The title of the *TIME* story, "The Mindful Revolution: The Science of Finding Focus in a Stressed Out, Multitasking Culture," really hits home how beneficial the practice of mindfulness can be and why it is so necessary in our lives. Stress is common, often accompanying us through our lives. Juggling multiple tasks, known as multitasking, creates a scattered mind. Mindfulness helps us manage stress and regain our ability to focus.

Mindfulness as an Essential Skill for the 21st Century

For some, mindfulness is viewed as a critical component to successfully navigating the demands of living in the 21st century. I've heard Kabat-Zinn, when interviewed about how he defines mindfulness, add a fourth component to his definition—paying attention on purpose, in the present moment, non-judgmentally, *and* as if your life depended on it.[6] Because, Kabat-Zinn argues, the quality of your life experience does depend on whether mindfulness is part of it. If our day is spent constantly racing and switching between tasks, we find ourselves feeling fragmented and fatigued by the end of the day. Or, if we spend our day worrying about something that has happened or about something that may occur if we are not vigilant, we also end the day feeling worn out and perhaps with even more heightened anxiety from not having focused on the tasks and opportunities the day brought to us. By bringing ourselves to the present moment repeatedly throughout our day, we can experience what is going on with more clarity and a true engagement with our lives.

There's been a shift in recent years from the value placed on how many things we can juggle simultaneously to how well we can engage in one task and direct all our attention to one thing at any given time. Multitasking is no longer the must-have skill it was perceived as being in the 1980s. Further, brain research suggests multitasking is a myth. Instead of simultaneously focusing on several things at one time, research has demonstrated that the brain is constantly shifting from task to task. While this shift may be imperceptible, it creates a level of fragmentation in attentional capacity. Worse still, it trains your mind to be good at jumping between tasks rather than developing the skill of sustained attention directed toward one task. The tremendous growth of technology has fostered this easily distractible state of mind by having at our fingertips a new bright and shiny object to shift attention to at any given moment. It takes considerable mental discipline to maintain attention on the task at hand in the face of an inexhaustible supply of information available to us at the touch of a keystroke.

In addition to training ourselves, albeit inadvertently, to have a distractible mind, our fast-paced, technologically-driven society is associated with high levels of anxiety and stress. Our minds wander from the present to the past or future, leading to worry about past mistakes or rumination about what the future may hold for us. With the catchy title, "A wandering mind is an unhappy mind," Harvard psychology researchers Killingsworth and Gilbert published a paper in the prestigious journal *Science* about the proclivity of the human mind to wander.[7] The researchers used a mobile phone app to track perceptions of happiness while people were engaged in different parts of their day. They found that people spend 46.9% of their waking hours thinking about something other than what they are doing—and that such mind-wandering typically makes them unhappy. Killingsworth and Gilbert concluded that the ability of the human mind to be other than in the present is a cognitive achievement that comes at a significant emotional cost.

The argument is not that reflections on the past or curious exploration of an idea for the future have no place in our experience. Rather, our constantly shifting attention *away* from the present and to the past or future means we can have under-developed skills of being where our bodies always and only are—in the present moment.

In addition to the emotional cost of a wandering mind that Killingsworth and Gilbert wrote about, the implications for high performance of the mind not being on task are, at the very minimum, significant. In some scenarios, these implications can become life-threatening. When you work at the extreme edges of challenge and skill, paying attention to what is happening is a non-negotiable. Alex Honnold, during the final pitch of Greenland's Ingmikortilaq, said this:

> *The most important part of climbing the wall for me is just staying in the moment. You know, just focusing on each task at hand, and not thinking about the scale of the wall in front of us. Not thinking about what might happen. Really you just have to focus on*

"Can I do this move?" And just take it one move at a time all the way to the top.[8]

Alex describes a focus that kept him and his climbing partner, Hazel, alive during their treacherous ascent of Ingmikortilaq. Alex stretches the boundaries of what is possible in human performance, and what he said here gives an insight into how he does so. While few of us will attempt to stretch our limits on the scale that Alex Honnold does, we can all improve our performance and our enjoyment on the tasks that matter to us. Learning how to focus attention on the present is the gift that mindfulness gives us. As well as enhancing attention and concentration, hundreds of research studies have associated mindfulness with many other benefits. These include reduction of stress and anxiety, improvement in mood and well-being, long-term effects on brain function—and even brain structure, and increased enjoyment through re-learning how to be present. Another benefit, less well-understood until recently, is facilitating flow.

How Mindfulness Facilitates Flow: Scientific Evidence

Bringing a mindful approach to a challenging task creates the opportunity for flow to occur. This has been a wonderful realization for me, to find a psychological skill that has so many benefits, including facilitating flow. Over the past 10-15 years, researchers have begun to look at relationships between mindfulness and flow and found empirical support for mindfulness facilitating flow. This is probably related to several skills that mindfulness cultivates, including present-moment focus, suspension of judgment, and acceptance of what is happening. I'll next share a few of the research findings where mindfulness and flow have been examined together.

Researchers Kee and Wang (2008) found an association between being mindful and self-reported flow in college athletes.[9] These researchers found that athletes scoring high in mindfulness also scored significantly higher in the flow dimensions of challenge-skill balance, clear goals, concentration on the task at hand, sense of control, and loss of self-consciousness. In another study, Moore (2013) found support for both cognitive flexibility and mindfulness in predicting the disposition to experience flow.[10]

Through using multidimensional measures of both flow and mindfulness, researchers Cathcart, McGregor, and Groundwater (2014) were able to examine the association between mindfulness and flow at a more detailed level.[11] They found that the flow dimension of total focus on the task at hand was demonstrated to be key to the association between mindfulness and flow. Correlations were found between this flow dimension and several of the mindfulness sub-scale dimensions, including the qualities known as describing, acting with awareness, and nonjudging of inner experience.

A recent study published in the journal *Psychology of Consciousness* (2023) found, with a sample of over 1600 participants, positive associations between scores on mindfulness scales and a measure of flow called deep, effortless concentration (DEC), leading the study authors to conclude that individuals who were more mindful tended to experience flow more often.[12] The researchers also found that individuals who were more mindful were more likely to experience flow (DEC) in a laboratory computer task. It is exciting to see the beginnings of experimental work investigating how mindfulness and flow are related.

Research examining relationships between mindfulness and flow will help deepen our understanding of how these two concepts are related. In addition to the development of experimental research such as the study outlined above, interventions where participants are trained in skills relevant to mindfulness and flow, and evaluating the impacts of such trainings, will help connect research to practice. A 2024 study illustrates the potential for research to translate to practical application.

With national-level archers from Hong Kong, Lo and colleagues (2024) implemented an online mindfulness training program and assessed scores on mindfulness, flow, and self-confidence questionnaires before and after the intervention. After the 12-week program, scores on mindfulness, flow, and self-confidence all increased. Mindfulness and flow, flow and self-confidence, and mindfulness and self-confidence were all positively related to each other.[13]

Insights from mindfulness research that explores what is happening in the brain are starting to uncover more clues about how mindfulness might facilitate flow. In one study published in the prestigious *Nature Reviews Neurosciences* journal, researchers reviewed an array of studies that showed differences in brain structure and function associated with meditation. One of the main conclusions drawn by the study authors about why mindfulness meditation is beneficial also points to how it facilitates flow—by decreasing the evaluative, self-focused perceptions known as self-referential processing while increasing present-moment awareness:

> *The findings from these studies have been taken to suggest that mindfulness meditation might alter the self-referential mode, so that a previous narrative, evaluative form of self-referential processing is replaced by greater awareness. We suggest that this shift in self-awareness is one of the major active mechanisms of the beneficial effects of mindfulness meditation.*[14]

One of the most important skills developed through training in mindfulness is greater self-awareness. And with this increased self-awareness comes an ability to recognize when the mind is getting caught up in unhelpful self-talk (self-referential processing). Over time and with repeated practice, an increasing aptitude is developed in letting go of this internal dialogue and re-focusing to the present. Letting go of an unhelpful mindset and replacing it with one grounded in the present sets the stage for flow. In a situation where the key pre-condition to flow is met—a challenging situation involving a high level of skills—an individual who has trained their mind to let go of thinking and to focus on the presenting task has considerable potential to experience flow.

The combination of having developed expertise in one's area of performance and an ability to be mindful is a powerful combination for facilitating flow. This was supported in a recent neuroimaging study looking at how the brain achieves a creative flow state. Rosen and colleagues, examining brain activity in jazz improvisation, found support for their hypothesis that flow results from the combination of expertise and a letting go of executive brain control.[15] The study involved hooking up jazz guitar players of low and high experience to EEGs and asking them to improvise to jazz lead sheets. Flow was assessed with one of the flow scales I developed called the Core Flow State Scale.[16] EEGs were examined to assess the areas of the brain associated with high (vs. low) flow improvisations. In high-flow performances, parts of the brain associated with the senses of hearing and touch were activated, while there was decreased activity in a region of the brain associated with executive control. This supported the "letting go" hypothesis. In neuroscience language, this is referred to as transient hypofrontality. There was also reduced activity in what is called the default mode network, an area of the brain associated with mind wandering and self-referential thinking. The expertise part of the hypothesis was supported by these patterns of brain activity being found in the high experience musicians, and not the musicians with less experience. The authors concluded that creative flow was enabled by extensive practice paired with reduced cognitive control.

The finding from this research of a letting go of cognitive control of what is happening in the brain in flow supports the premises of mindfulness (and ACT). The notion that thinking less and instead becoming immersed in the present moment can be beneficial is supported by extensive research in mindfulness and with ACT. Combining present-moment awareness with skilled performance facilitates flow. Through engaging in mindfulness practices and developing skills so we avoid getting caught up in thinking, flow moves from being perceived as a wonderful but somewhat random experience to an attainable state. The next chapter will describe some foundational mindfulness practices that may help you in your quest to find flow.

CHAPTER 8

Practical Mindfulness Strategies for Finding Flow

So, I did a classic extreme climber thing of jumping in the deep end. My first experience of meditation was on a 10-day silent Vipassana retreat. I was just like, "Oh, my God, this is the living end. I will never survive this!" But then, at the end of it, you know, my mind was very still, very calm, very present. I could sit for like an hour at a time, which is pretty mad. You know, that you can go from being so distracted to being still.

—*Hazel Findlay*

Hazel found through her first intrepid 10-day silent retreat a shift from perceiving she could not survive it to enjoying the experience of her mind being still, calm, and present. From my first experiences with yoga nidra, where I experienced a profound shift in my level of awareness, practicing meditation has been an enjoyable experience. I love going deep into a relaxed state through practices like yoga nidra and Western-based body scans. Equally, I am grateful to have learned how to mindfully come to my breathing in a moment of unwanted heightened stress.

I often get asked what the difference is between mindfulness and meditation. They are similar terms and are often used interchangeably. One distinction that I like to refer to is that meditation can be viewed as the formal practice of mindfulness. Remembering that mindfulness is how we pay attention: on purpose, in the present moment, and non-judgmentally. We can pay attention this way in a formal meditation practice. We can also remember to be mindful as we go through our day. This latter can be thought of as the informal practice of mindfulness—using cues in our day to refocus back to the present moment. Developing skills in both formal mindfulness (meditation) practices and informal mindfulness practices create brain pathways conducive to flow.

Learning to Meditate

In the times we live in, with heightened awareness about the benefits of mindfulness, most of us will get exposed to the practice in some way as adults. As awareness of the benefits of the practice grows, there is also an increasing number of schools bringing mindfulness to students from a young age. This wasn't the case in the 1950s. However, one lucky six-year-old developed his skills in mindfulness when he was taught meditation by a teacher employed to help him with a stuttering problem. John Hendry, who has been awarded an Order of Australia (OAM) medal for his lifelong work as an educator (and another OAM as a coach), began life in a small town in regional Victoria, Australia. Experiencing stuttering from a young age, his parents sent him on a 4-hour train trip to Melbourne for weekly tutoring from an educator who specialized in helping children with stuttering. John shared with me how he could not pronounce *S* or *N* as a six-year-old. His weekly lessons involved meditation and singing—very innovative for the 1950s.

From the ages of 6 to 13, John was taught how to focus on a task and how to speak without stuttering through learning meditation and singing. While John didn't become a singer, he did become a life-long meditator. He credits this practice with enabling him to quiet the distraction he experienced in his mind about his stutter and instead learn to focus on the task and experience flow. As John said to me, through meditation, he was able to get rid of the stutter on the S. And then the N.

John went on to teach meditation to the thousands of students who had the good fortune to come under his tutelage. John shared with me that for the 50 years in his teaching and Director of Student Welfare roles, he began every lesson with a 2-minute meditation. While this may not have been unusual in the 2000s, it was not the norm in 1969, when John first began teaching. John shared with me that he told his students that he didn't want them to waste any time in the lesson, telling them, *"This is really important—you will never have this 40 minutes again in your life."* And so, each lesson began with a short meditation to get them focused for that lesson. John's message to the students was not only that the lesson's 40 minutes would be lost if attention was not acute, but also that each student carried with them what John called "grey noise." Grey noise consisted of brain thoughts that were forever present and drew students away from paying attention. Meditation enabled them to quiet that grey noise and reduce, if not stop, such distraction. Students recognized the "grey noise" and that it inhibited engagement. Such a valuable lesson to learn from a young age in terms of future propensity to find flow.

John shared how the 2-minute meditation helped the students to experience focused engagement—and helped him as their teacher to get into flow. John recounted how students would often jokingly say to him, *"Times up, Sir!"* to remind him that a class period had ended, as John would get so absorbed in each lesson he taught that time literally disappeared for him. John credits his ability to get into flow in his teaching directly to having learned meditation from a young age.

Meditation practices can be as short as the time it takes for one complete breath or as long as you want a practice to be. The practice can be guided by a class teacher or via one of a myriad of meditation apps. Over time, you may become your own guide, and there are certainly advantages to being able to take yourself through a practice. For example, in the midst of a stressful workday, you may not be able to pull out your phone and play a guided meditation. However, regardless of whether you have an app on hand, you can always bring awareness to your breathing and regulate your arousal level by focusing attention on the breath.

Breathing Awareness

Breathing techniques are the foundation for all mindfulness practices, both the formal practice (meditation) and the informal practice. I've found that there is so much scope to improve how we breathe, making it a powerful tool for creating positive change in our experience. While we are, of course, breathing all the time we are alive, without a deliberate focus on *how* we are breathing, we may not only be breathing inefficiently but also missing a simple way to improve our health and longevity.

If we only have so many breaths in a lifetime, doesn't it make sense to slow the breathing down? A common problem among people who have not trained their breathing is taking too many breaths in a minute. Once we learn the skill of breathing slowly and fully, we may literally be positively influencing our longevity! And we most certainly will change our immediate experience for the better by bringing calm to our nervous system with each long, slow breath we take. Try it now: breathe slowly and deeply for five consecutive breaths and see whether you experience a change in your experience. Most people report that bringing deliberate awareness to their breathing and focusing on breathing slowly and deeply creates calm in their system, physically and emotionally. This attention to breathing can become a cue to help you step into a flow state.

Breathing is foundational to meditation practices. If you want to keep a meditation practice simple, spend some time each day focusing on slow, deep breathing. You could start with 5 minutes/day and build up the practice to, say, 15 minutes. And there you have it—you would now be practicing meditation! Sounds simple, right? The breathing part of it is. However, the mind will likely have something to say about your being still and focusing on your breath. Most likely, your mind will tell you that there are much more interesting and/or important things for you to be doing than focusing on your breathing. And your mind may be right. The skill comes in deciding whether it is OK to ignore the stories your mind is telling you and to remain focused on the breathing. That is where practice starts to become really valuable—to notice the mind chatter and bring your attention back to the breath. Perhaps again, and again, and again. Each time you practice this way, you are training your mind to notice when it has drifted off from a present moment focus and bring it back—to the present, to what is happening in your body with your breathing. Over time, you will find that you get better at noticing when your mind has wandered and in bringing your focus back to the present more effortlessly.

This skill of noticing when your mind has wandered and bringing it back to the present is part of most meditation practices. And it is centrally relevant to what Kabat-Zinn refers to in his definition of mindfulness as paying attention non-judgmentally. Learning to bring the attention back without self-criticism about how, for example, your mind has wandered yet again is going to allow you to improve your mindfulness more effectively than berating yourself for not being able to keep your attention on your breath. Or giving up the practice because your mind is so full of thoughts. In group discussions on mindfulness, it is not uncommon to hear someone say that while they can see the benefits of mindfulness, it is not for them—their mind is too busy, too full of thoughts. It's often only upon starting to meditate that such a realization comes into awareness and might be the reason for giving up. However, a busy mind is what most of us have, or at least what we start with before engaging with meditation. And everyone can improve their ability to focus through practice. I encourage you to give it a good try, starting with a simple 5 minutes a day of focusing on slow, deep breathing, bringing attention back to the breathing each time you notice your mind wandering. You may even find that you look forward to these times of relative stillness in the mind and that your practice naturally grows into longer times spent in this critically important practice of breathing meditation.

The long exhale
Bringing awareness to breathing is the first step in a breathing meditation practice. Once aware of your breathing, the next step is to deliberately slow the breathing down. Important here is to focus on the exhale, following the exhalation all the way to the end of each breath out. It is our exhalation that often gets compromised when we are anxious or simply inefficient in our breathing. We might even remember being instructed to "take a deep breath" by someone observing our heightened anxiety level. Taking a deep breath *in* is only half the story, or breath cycle. More important to regulating stress levels is a long, slow exhalation. It is the exhalation that signals to the brain to activate the relaxation response in the body. Conversely, a deep breath in, followed by a short or incomplete exhale, signals the brain of a potential threat. This can then lead to more expression of stress in the body, such as rapid breathing, elevated heart rate, and other fight-or-flight responses. Long, slow exhalations can calm this elevated response down, allow us to think more clearly, and take appropriate next actions.

The 4-part breath
Another practice that trains us to slow down our breathing and to ensure the exhale is not ignored is 4-part breathing. Often referred to as box breathing, it is a popular practice for many. I think part of the reason for its popularity is that the practice gives the mind a constant and repetitive point of focus. It involves mentally counting 1,2,3,4 for each part of the breath cycle: breath in, pause, breath out, pause. It is called box breathing because each breath is made up of four equal parts, and one might be encouraged to imagine each part of the breath as one

side of a square or box. It is more important in this practice to focus on gradually lengthening your own breath cycle according to your individual starting point—rather than striving to achieve a breath cycle that visibly resembles a box by trying too hard to achieve equal emphasis on the four parts that make up each cycle.

A variation to 4-part breathing is to gradually lengthen the exhale over several rounds of breathing. Once again, the breath is counted, both in-breath and out-breath. Once a pattern of counting is established, the next step is to lengthen the exhale by a count each breath cycle, until you reach a sustainable count with the exhale, which is longer than each inhale. Similar to the focus on a long exhale, this counting and gradually extending the exhale strengthens your breathing, activates the relaxation response, and gives your mind a specific focus through attention to the counting process. It is all about training the mind to be in the present, remembering that it is in the present that flow is found.

Lengthening the breathing practice
Having a specific focus point, such as the long exhale or counting the breathing, gives the mind something tangible to focus on and thus provides a deterrent to the wandering mind. As one develops a breathing meditation practice, lengthening the time of practice is one way to keep progressing. A longer practice ups the challenge, and thus, using counting can help keep the mind focused for longer periods of time. Counting the breath back from a chosen starting point is a technique used in many yoga nidra practices. For example, starting at 21 (or any number of your choosing), one is guided to start with mentally counting "21" for the in-breath and then 21 again for the out-breath. Followed by 20-20, 19-19, and so on. The structure of this practice is useful for keeping focus, and the natural rhythm of the breathing is also soothing to the nervous system.

Alternate nostril breathing

Another breathing practice drawn from yoga that is both calming and focusing is alternate nostril breathing. It is a popular practice in yoga classes that incorporate *pranayama* or breathing exercises, so readers who attend yoga may be familiar with this practice. The process involves gently closing off one nostril while breathing through the other. Commencing with breathing in the left nostril, then out the right nostril, followed by breathing in the right nostril and out the left nostril. And so the practice continues, with the right nostril being gently closed by the thumb of the right hand, and the left nostril by the ring finger of the left hand. The first and second fingers of the right hand gently press on the midpoint of the forehead, a point referred to in yoga as the eyebrow center. While it might sound a bit complicated, once familiar with the process, participants find it beneficial and enjoyable. Closing off a nostril creates a lengthened breath through the open nostril, and both inhale and exhale are given equal emphasis.

The breathing practices that I've described here have the following features in common: lengthening the breath cycle, and in particular, lengthening the exhale; rhythm and ease in breathing; and incorporating a focus point for the mind.

Developing breathing practices provides an important foundational skill for all other meditation practices and is thus a great place to begin—or develop—a practice. Breathing practices have also been shown to improve physical health and, in particular, respiratory health. There are some excellent books written on the health benefits of breathing, including Nestor's bestseller, *Breath: The New Science of a Lost Art*. Nestor extensively studied the science of breathing well for his book and concluded that breathing is a missing pillar of good health.[1]

The importance of breathing effectively for both mental and physical well-being can't be over-emphasized. And the practice of mindful breathing is simple—but not necessarily easy to do. However, with some practice, the benefits you can experience will lead to greater awareness and more ease in keeping attention on the breath. Mindful breathing is part of the routine of high-level performers seeking flow in what they do. So, too, is the next foundational mindfulness practice, body awareness.

Body Awareness

Athletes and performing artists rely on their bodies to perform and recognize the importance of physical preparation and readiness to their craft. Having the appropriate amount of energy, or arousal, in the body for the demands of the task is integral to successful performance in all domains. Knowing what the appropriate level of energy is comes with good body awareness. This is developed through practices that bring attention to the body, and in particular, noticing where there is unwanted tension in parts of the body. The mindful practice of taking awareness systematically through the body, often referred to as a body scan, is an important one to help with self-regulation of arousal levels.

Body scans

For many people who practice meditation, body scans are a favorite practice because they can be associated with deep levels of relaxation. Body scan practices have a long history in Western health practices. In the 1920s, Edmund Jacobsen developed a technique he called *Progressive Muscle Relaxation (PMR)*.[2] This practice, which continues to be popular today, involves systematically working through parts of the body, first tensing and then relaxing muscle groups. Another earlier pioneer in relaxation practices was a physician called Herbert Benson, who, in the 1960s, developed and promoted a relaxation practice that was also grounded in body scans. Benson referred to his practice as the *Relaxation Response*, also the title of his subsequent book, in which he described the health benefits of a systematic body-focused relaxation.[3] Some of these benefits included lowered blood pressure and heart rate and decreased stress levels in general.

Yoga nidra

There are a variety of meditation practices that focus on body awareness and relaxing the body by focusing on levels of tension and relaxation in muscle groups. One of the reasons body scan practices tend to be enjoyable is because they provide a progressive set of tangible cues to focus on and result in physical as well as mental relaxation. The early yogis recognized this, and thousands of years ago, the powerful body-based practice of yoga nidra was developed. As mentioned earlier, yoga nidra was always the favorite part of any yoga classes that I have attended. The styles of yoga that incorporate a yoga nidra practice generally have classes end on this lovely approach to relaxation and awareness. There was one class I attended for a year when living interstate, where the instructor began *and* ended the yoga class with a yoga nidra practice. I found that starting a yoga session with yoga nidra brought me into my body and out of my overthinking mind. This then led to a strong connection with the physical practice of the class. And then another yoga nidra practice to finish the class led to profound levels of relaxation. It was both the deep levels of relaxation and the enhanced body awareness that I gained in these practices that became the driving force behind my seeking to undertake yoga teacher training.

Body-based meditation practices can be learned in a yoga class or through a psychologist or other therapist trained in bodywork. These practices are useful for everyone to help develop awareness of physical tension and strategies for releasing it. For anyone who finds anxiety a constant companion, body-based practices help to bring about increased levels of relaxation and a letting go of tension held in the body.

Sometimes, our main experience of tension and anxiety may be in the mind—our body may be relatively relaxed, but our mind can be racing. This is where mindfulness practices that focus on developing awareness of our thoughts and effective ways of quieting the mind can provide another pathway to flow.

Letting Go of Thoughts

A key goal in meditation is to bring awareness to the present moment and to let go of the constant stream of thoughts that tend to occupy our minds in waking states. The goal is not, as is sometimes misconstrued, to have an empty mind. Rather, it is to have an awareness of what we are focused on and to bring the mind back to the present when it inevitably strays to past or future thinking. What do we bring the attention back to? The breathing, the body, to sounds we hear—to something that is grounded in the present. By bringing attention to one of our senses, we break the stream of thinking that takes us away from the present.

Learning to be more aware of the information coming to us through our senses is one of the gifts mindfulness provides. We start our lives as sensing beings, but as we grow and become educated, thinking takes priority over sensing. Our thoughts can have little or nothing to do with what is happening in the present moment. However, we often give considerable weight to our thoughts, regardless of whether they are grounded in reality or not. As we train in mindfulness, we return to recognizing the valuable information our senses provide. Jon Kabat-Zinn emphasized the importance of paying attention to the information we receive from our senses with one of his books, aptly titled *Coming to Our Senses*.

A meditation practice that is designed to train our skill in letting go of thoughts might incorporate a visual image of thoughts being let go, such as placing thoughts on clouds and letting them drift by. Visual cues to let go of a thought can be paired with a verbal cue, such as "tree it" or "park it." Immediately, as the thought is released from attention, a present-moment cue is engaged. Often, the cue is breathing awareness because it is simple and a constant. The process of letting go of thoughts is one that generally requires repetition and persistence in bringing attention to the present. This is because we have learned to perceive our thoughts as defining our identity, leading to a lack of space between ourselves and our thinking.

A similar process is used to let go of painful memories or images that arise or strong emotions that are unhelpful to our situation. When memories or emotions are difficult to engage with, it is best to do these practices under the guidance of an experienced practitioner, often a psychologist with a special interest in mindfulness.

Integrative Meditative Practices

Having spent many years in university settings, it was helpful to experience the richness of learnings available through ancient wisdom traditions. My mindfulness teaching and practice have been informed both by Eastern meditative practices such as yoga nidra and Western practices that have been grounded in more empirical approaches. One approach that I particularly like integrates the ancient yoga nidra practice with Western-based psychology. It is called Integrative Restoration (iRest) Yoga Nidra and was developed by clinical psychologist Dr. Richard Miller.[4] I've had the opportunity to undertake teacher training with Richard and to experience the deeply meditative experience that iRest provides.

The practice of iRest involves several steps and integrates breathing, body awareness, being with thoughts and emotions, and arriving at a place of simply being. The latter is referred to in other types of practices as open awareness. Unlike most other meditation practices, when the goal is "simply being" or being in open awareness, there is no specific object of focus (such as the breath or awareness of the body). Richard Miller refers to this meditative experience as resting in awareness, with the goal of experiencing equanimity. This is quite the other end of the spectrum to our notions of productivity through "doing" and doing more. My experience in iRest yoga nidra practices, and through teaching these practices, is that states of deep rest, acceptance of experience,

Mantra Music as a Pathway to Flow

and enjoyment of being in the present moment can all be attained. These experiences can lead us to flow.

Music, for me, has always been an escape from a continual stream of analytical thinking. And listening to my favorite music, especially at live concerts, has been one way for me to find flow. My preferred music is rock, and thus, I was surprised to be taken in by the meditative devotional music of the Australian duo Prem and Jethro of Sacred Earth.[5] I was writing a piece on their work as Australia's leading artists in the ambient music genre for the yoga journal *Australian Yoga Life*.[6] Having attended a live Sacred Earth event prior to my interview with Prem and Jethro, I had experienced first-hand how their music transported me to deeper aspects of myself, and I found myself getting totally absorbed in their music. It was a deeply meditative experience for me, and so I decided to focus on that as I prepared questions for the interview. We talked about finding stillness through music and how important it was to be able to touch into stillness in our frenetic lives. Jethro helped me understand how it was that I felt a deep sense of connection with their music and with myself, as he explained,

> *Our music evokes emotion, that is, feeling an emotion in this moment without having to connect it with memory or some past emotional feeling. No story is attached to it, unlike songs we hear on the radio.*

Prem and Jethro shared how they came to connect with stillness in their music. It was through the times they spent playing in markets that they learned to *"sit in that clear, quiet space"* amidst all the bustle and noise going on around them. *"We had to learn to sit in stillness with all the noise and present our music harmoniously."* By not fighting the challenging market experience, they were able to connect with a place of stillness within. In further explaining their ability to develop stillness in what they do, Prem related back to their training ground at the markets: *"It came from all those years sitting on the street, in that constant noise, learning how to hold that space."*

Hearing how Prem and Jethro described their music experience, I mentioned the flow experience to them during our interview. I could see that Prem and Jethro immediately connected with the concept. For example, Prem spoke of what being in flow while performing meant for her:

> *For me, there is a flow when I am able to stay centered, and I am aware of all the notes Jethro is playing. There is a harmony between our musical communication and our energetic communication. When I feel our hearts are connected, I feel our music is moving out in a way that is harmonious.*

Prem spoke about one of the most rewarding characteristics of flow during a concert, which is being free of the shackles of time:

> *In concerts, time does not even exist for me. A song that goes for 10 minutes seems to have a timelessness; it could have been going for 3 minutes or 25 minutes. I think a lot of people feel that too, at our concerts. They are always surprised that it has been three hours.*

How music can be meditation and a pathway to flow, was evident in speaking to these two musicians. Prem and Jethro explained to me that their work and their lives were about retaining an inner calmness, equanimity, and flow.

I hope that by sharing some foundational mindfulness practices, I have been able to demonstrate how these practices train our attention to be in the present moment. It is in the present moment that we find flow. Thus, the benefits of practicing mindfulness extend from known psychological outcomes to the perhaps lesser-known one of facilitating flow.

In the next chapter, I focus on two mindfulness proponents who have brought to the world of elite professional sport awareness of mindfulness as a pathway to flow.

CHAPTER 9

How Two Mindfulness Whisperers Helped Unlock Flow on the Basketball Court

Phil Jackson Brings Awareness of Flow to the NBA

While spending a sabbatical working with Mike at the University of Chicago in 1997, I learned about the legendary Chicago Bulls NBA team. I was living on campus at the University of Chicago and remember the experience of watching the Bulls win their 5th NBA title. The final series with the Utah Jazz was captivating, with the teams swapping the lead, but with the Bulls ultimately victorious. The energy in Chicago was high, and I became a fan of the Bulls and their team of strong personalities. I was also aware of the strong, mostly calm, presence of their coach, Phil Jackson. I came across a book Jackson had written about his coaching philosophy at the University of Chicago bookstore—*Sacred Hoops.*

Reading *Sacred Hoops* helped me to understand the calm presence of Phil Jackson on the court and the strong team spirit of the Bulls. In the book, I encountered for the first time a coach who focused his coaching toward mindset in an openly spiritual way. Jackson was a proponent of mindfulness and included meditation exercises in training the Bulls. He instilled in the players strategies to be clearly focused, in the moment, and to remain calm in the chaos of a fast-moving basketball game. Jackson describes how, through working with the Bulls on mindfulness strategies—both for his players and for himself—the athletes played better and were more likely to find flow as a team. They played in a more self-determined way, as Jackson describes:

> *And the joy they experience working in harmony is a powerful motivating force that comes from deep within, not from some frenzied coach pacing along the sidelines, shouting obscenities into the air.*[1]

I love the way Jackson described how his coaching style differed from the norm in the NBA. Jackson taught his players how to tap into their inner selves and into flow, as illustrated in the next quote, which also captures the beauty of this experience:

> *What makes basketball so exhilarating is the joy of losing yourself completely in the dance, even if it's just for one beautiful, transcendent moment.*[2]

This idea of losing yourself completely in the dance describes aspects of several flow dimensions: action-awareness merging, total concentration, loss of self-consciousness, and autotelic experience.

Jackson worked with all the players to develop mindfulness and flow-readiness. However, with Michael Jordan, there was something special already there, a physical and mental skill set that set him apart from his peers. Jackson described how Jordan's ability to stay calm and focused on the court was unmatched and how he thrived on the frenzied action of the game:

> *He loves being in the center of a storm. While everyone else is spinning madly out of control, he moves effortlessly across the floor, enveloped by a great stillness.*[3]

Such an eloquent way to describe a player in flow. Anyone who has watched Jordan play basketball will know that sense of Jordan seemingly playing in his own impenetrable world while everyone else on the court appeared to be racing and exerting what looked like far more effort.

It wasn't just the players who found flow on the court, with Jackson describing how his own experience coaching during a game was one of coming alive, where *"time slows down and I experience the blissful feeling of being totally engaged in the action."*[4] Knowing about flow makes it more likely for one to get into flow. In this quote, Jackson describes how he became totally engaged in the action on the court, finding flow while coaching the fast-paced, high-stress sport of pro basketball.

The pathway to flow for player and coach, as described by Jackson in *Sacred Hoops,* was an ability to become immersed in the present moment. This skill we call mindfulness was one that seemed to come naturally to Jordan, and it was part of Jackson's skill set when he arrived at the Bulls, facilitating his focusing on it as a key skill for the team to develop. It was an approach to life Jackson had grown up with, being raised in a spiritually focused family, which influenced him as a coach to explore practices that cultivated awareness and presence. These two qualities were important to Jackson's unparalleled success as a coach in the NBA and to his developing flow-ready players.

While Jackson was very familiar with, and adroit in, the practice of mindfulness, he chose to bring in a mindfulness coach to work specifically with the players on this skill in the 1993-94 season.

Performance Whisperer George Mumford

George Mumford was an excellent choice, having played basketball competitively, roomed with Dr. J (Julius Erving), having experienced, in his words, "life in the 'hood,'" and having transformed his life from a place of substance addiction to one where mindfulness became a solid component of his life. George's business is aptly named "Eye of the Hurricane."

In his book *Unlocked: Embrace your Greatness, Find the Flow, Discover Success,* George described how he has taught mindfulness to the most elite of NBA basketball players and to people from all walks of life, including life-sentence prison inmates. George refers to his best meditation students as being the two greatest basketball players he ever worked with, Michael Jordan and Kobe Bryant—as well as the double-lifers in prison.[5] Such different lives and as big a contrast in life trajectory as one could expect between two demographics. Perhaps both a super-successful NBA star and a prisoner who is going to see out their days inside a cell, are both seeking stillness within. For the basketball player, to find focus and calm amidst the chaos of celebrity life and the chaos on the court. For the lifer, meditation might give some level of peace and calm to an unimaginably hard life.

George had been working with the Chicago Bulls for over a year before Jordan's second return to the NBA in 1995. George described in *Unlocked* that he wasn't sure how Jordan would respond to the regular meditation sessions he had been holding with the players. He remarked how in the very first mindfulness practice MJ attended, he just dropped right into a meditative state. Just like he would drop into a flow state on the court. MJ was a truly gifted athlete, physically and mentally.

The clause MJ insisted on having included in his 1995 return to the NBA demonstrates an autotelic personality, or someone prone to experience flow. The famous "love of the game clause" that Jordan had written into his return-to-NBA contract enabled him to play basketball anytime, anywhere, with whomever he wanted. Most NBA players had to curtail their play outside of team basketball to avoid injury. Jordan wanted no such restrictions, and instead insisted that he be able to play the game he so loved whenever he wanted.

During his stellar career with the LA Lakers, the late Kobe Bryant was similar to Jordan in his love for the game. Kobe also demonstrated an indomitable mastery perspective, training harder and longer than his peers. While extremely competitive, Kobe demonstrated being motivated by self-mastery. Remembering back to the chapter on mastery and flow, losing means very different things depending on whether one is motivated by self-improvement or ego. I heard an interview with Kobe about what losing meant to him, and he described it as exciting, as it means you have different things to get better at—a classic mastery outlook. Both MJ and Kobe offer model illustrations of a mastery perspective.

In another interview, Kobe was presented with two types of players—players who love to win and players who hate to lose. On being asked which type he was, Kobe replied that he was neither. He went on to say,

> *I play to figure things out; I play to learn something. If you play with a fear of failure or you play with the will to win, I think it's a weakness either way. If you find common ground in the middle, in the center, then it doesn't matter. You're unfazed by either. It enables you to stay in the moment, stay connected to it, and not feel anything except what's in front of you.*[6]

There's so much in this quote by Kobe Bryant. There is clear evidence that being at the top of one's sport as a professional athlete doesn't necessarily translate to an ego orientation. The love of the game can continue to be the primary motivator, even in the face of fame and millions of dollars coming your way as a successful pro athlete. Staying in the moment while playing was the goal, and this required being unfazed by either winning or losing. Kobe describes in this quote an equanimity toward playing his sport.

Kobe's ability to stay completely present while he played allowed him to be very familiar with the experience of being in flow:

> *When you get in that zone, it's just a supreme confidence. Things just slow down. You really do not try to focus on what's going on because you can lose it*

> *in a second. You have to really try to stay in the present and not let anything break that rhythm.*[7]

Noting that the zone is a popular term to describe flow by athletes, the way Kobe describes what happens in this state with such detailed familiarity demonstrates how tuned into this state he was in his highly successful pro basketball career.

Kobe and MJ are clear examples of being motivated by autotelic or intrinsic factors. Kobe and MJ are also two of the strongest examples of athletes with an uncanny ability to stay focused and totally in the moment when playing. Playing for the love of the game and playing in flow are not independent, as I've tried to describe throughout this book. Mike (Csikszentmihalyi) certainly took this viewpoint, interchangeably using the terms flow and enjoyment in his writings.

In *Unlocked*, George Mumford makes a great distinction between peak performance and what he refers to as pure performance, which he uses to describe what being in flow is like. He contrasts performing at one's peak, which he argues is unsustainable, with the sustained excellence of pure performance:

> *In contrast, pure performance is about the quest for authenticity, which leads to purity of expression. There is no peak in pure performance because there is no limit to the possibilities that exist. Peak performance is stationary—a mountain summit. Pure performance is flow, carrying us along ceaselessly and constantly revealing new heights. Once we experience pure performance, we feel more fully ourselves, and we want more.*[8]

The way George has been able to link mindfulness and flow in some very public, high-profile settings has helped to make both concepts more mainstream. I had the opportunity to interview George about his ideas and his work during the writing of this book. Although we come from very different backgrounds, our respective exploration of flow and mindfulness provided a synchronicity to our discussion. George's work with a great diversity of people demonstrated to me how universal the benefits of mindfulness are and reinforced how special being in flow is to all who experience it.

George shared with me how he was able to teach MJ about flow and simultaneously, how MJ taught him about flow. Anyone who has seen Michael Jordan play will recognize that he is a classic example of flow in action. Famous Celtics player Larry Bird, commentating on a playoff game between the Celtics and the Bulls, in which Jordan scored 63 points, was famously quoted as saying, *"That wasn't Michael Jordan out there; that was God disguised as Michael Jordan."*

When describing pure performance, George referred to this quality as perhaps the most important part of what made MJ so great, as well as being a crucial part of what he taught Jordan and what Jordan taught him.[8] I asked George in our interview what he meant when he said that he taught MJ about flow and that MJ taught him about flow. George shared that one of his skills is the ability to take a complex subject and simplify it. He was able to explain to MJ how MJ was able to do what he did. Through this understanding, MJ was able to attain even higher levels of performance. MJ showed George how, in the midst of chaos and the challenge of elevating one's skills, someone can find quiet and focus and how this leads to flow. He noticed with MJ that *"the more chaotic it gets, the calmer he gets."* For George, MJ was the embodiment of what he was teaching, and working with him helps explain why his business is named "Eye of the Hurricane." George saw MJ as operating at a level all his own:

> *MJ had a tremendous amount of energy. It's about a certain level of what we call right effort. You go from an initial level of effort to get you out of low energy.*

Then the persistence to be able to struggle, and work through things. Then if you do that, you develop this ability to access invincibility, to access a higher power. Effortless effort.

MJ had this access. I could feel his calmness when I first met him. He was vibrating at a different level. We can talk about physical ability until the cows come home, but it's really about the attractor field. There's something about when you're at a certain energy or level of consciousness. At one level of consciousness, you have access to options that you don't have at another one. And so this is what I like to talk about, this idea of the eye of the hurricane. When you come out of that phase, there's a knowing, a wisdom and a creativity that expresses itself. All of a sudden, you're seeing things in different ways.

Probably anyone who has witnessed MJ fly toward the hoop might agree that he had access to a higher power! What George has been able to do, through his understanding of awareness, mindfulness, and flow, is to explain how Jordan moved his already exceptional standard of play to new levels of energy and focus that allowed him to tap into his greatness.

When he came in to work with the Bulls in 1993, George was given a brief by coach Phil Jackson—to help make his players flow-ready. In his book *Unlocked*, George described how he introduced flow to the players, highlighting the importance of mindfulness and challenging oneself:

> *"You've all had flow experiences," I told them. "I want to help you to have more of those. Mindfulness gets you flow-ready. If you try to get into flow, it*

> *won't happen. But if you just attend to the moment, and if your challenges are high, and your skills, knowledge, and experience are all also high, you will get there. It is a matter of continuing to push through and challenge yourself."*[9]

I like how George describes mindfulness as helping to make you flow-ready. I wholeheartedly agree with this, and since learning about and practicing mindfulness, I've found it to be such a valuable skill, including as a pathway to flow, as described in Chapter 7. George shared in our interview how mindfulness developed the players' ability to observe their experience in a non-critical way. He referred to how such pure awareness allows you to see things clearly and that it is accompanied by a slowing down of things, providing space between stimulus and response.

> *If you just watch things in the eye of the hurricane, you're just quiet. You slow things down; there is a space there. And in that space, you have the freedom and power to choose, like Viktor Frankl said. Thinking and action are aligned. You slow things down by not trying to grab anything, push anything away, or even try to interpret it. You just let it be. You get to the point where you form the intention and then you allow it to happen.*

George shared with me that while it can be hard to explain this process, what develops is a way of being. From forming an intention, to then getting out of the way, your mind figures things out and starts making connections that previously were not seen. The space in the chaos, which can also be thought of as the pause between stimulus and response, combined with trust in one's skills, allows great performance to happen.

In my interview with George, I asked him how he helped NBA basketball-winning teams increase the challenge when they were already playing at such a high level. George encouraged the players to be comfortable with being uncomfortable, to be focused on the continuous development of their potential, and to open the door to pure performance. "This allows us," George explained, "to transcend our limits again and again." In *Unlocked*, George described how pure performance is about *". . . the process of becoming, of self-discovery, of finding out what we're made of and who we really are."*[10]

George shared in our interview that the way Phil Jackson coached was to focus on constant improvement—of every aspect of a player, including their wellness. Winning was viewed by Jackson as a by-product of focusing on pure performance. The synergy between Jackson's growth-mindset approach to coaching and George's teaching the players mindfulness as a pathway to flow led to outstanding achievements on the basketball court. There were also high levels of enjoyment for both players and spectators, who were able to witness flow in action.

George's life is a model of flow in action. He shared with me in our interview that flow is his life:

> *Flow is the only way to go! I live a lot in flow. I am challenging myself. Not to get a goal. I see flow as a by-product of having clear goals and having a vision, purpose, and passion. To me, each moment is pregnant with possibility. I am still unlocking. The joy of discovery is so amazing.*

George has an optimistic view of humans and of the potential within each person. He talked with me about his aim of unlocking the masterpiece within each person he has the opportunity to connect with.

> *We all have this greatness within us, and if we embrace it and find our flow, we will discover success.*

And success is about honestly expressing yourself, having an intention, and being able to perform it, to express it, in a way where you feel good about it.

George's definition of success sums up key themes of this book: mastery perspective, clear goals, coming to the present moment, and trusting oneself to find flow. George has learned so much from his own life experiences and the opportunity to work with some of the best athletes on the planet. Both Phil Jackson and George Mumford brought their high levels of self-awareness and awareness of flow to the basketball court, where they (and we) were able to observe the effects of teaching disciplined performers about mindfulness and flow in action.

CHAPTER 10

Flow in the Information Age

Flow Becomes Somewhat Mainstream

When I first started researching flow in the late 1980s and early 1990s, the term *flow* was new to me, and yet it resonated with me right away, giving a name to experiences I did not previously have a language for. I have maintained my passion for talking and writing about this state, and I find that most people, once they are provided with a description of flow, can relate some of the most positive experiences in their lives to this state. It's great to work in an area where the focus is on positive states of being and to spread understanding of an experience so closely related to personal meaning and growth.

For many years, when asked what I studied, I would inevitably have to provide a definition or description of flow. I understood this, as I, too, was once unaware that there was a psychological concept that captured the best moments I'd experienced. I was, however, puzzled by what seemed to be a rise and fall in interest in flow, both in academic circles and in the popular press. I guess that I naively expected others to be as captivated with the concept as myself. But it wasn't just my own positive perceptions about flow—anyone I'd talk with about flow would echo how valuable an experience it was. I have never encountered a blank face when I explain what flow is. Rather, people experience an *aha* moment and often leap to share with me special flow experiences they've had.

Knowing how flow resonates with so many, it has been a bit puzzling to find a relative lack of attention to it in traditional psychology, as well as in most performance settings. I think there are probably several reasons for this. One is that flow is a subjective experiential state, inherently difficult to research. Advances in brain-body technologies are leading to an emerging understanding of what is happening within the body in flow. However, the need to be in a scientific laboratory for advanced physiological assessments of flow means that opportunities to tap into what is a somewhat elusive state for most are limited. It's generally not easy to drop into flow in a laboratory.

Music and gaming may be exceptions to this, and the study referred to in Chapter 8, with jazz guitarists improvising while having brain activity recorded, illustrates the possibility of examining flow in a lab setting. Also, as technological advances continue, improvements with in-situ recordings of brain activity and physiological activation will help expand a neuropsychological understanding of flow.

I have, somewhat sadly, encountered people who have sought to minimize the relevance of flow, either through not clearly understanding what flow is or viewing it as not as important as other areas of psychological study, perhaps citing *their* area of interest as more important to study, understand, or experience. I remain as convinced today as I was as a young academic about the significance of studying flow despite challenges from people who, at times, seem to be pushing their own research or political agenda. Through his writings, Mike has provided a richness to the understanding of human experience that is unique in psychology. Though the impact of his work has been remarkably broad, this has occurred through the genius of his ideas and not through any self-promotion. As has been described by those who knew him best, Mike was a humble scholar and preferred to let his ideas speak for themselves. In a competitive and technologically-driven world, where ideas are often promoted through large-scale exposure across whatever platforms are available, flow has unfortunately not garnered the same level of attention as some other psychological concepts.

While psychology has not taken up the study of flow to the extent that I think the concept deserves, the awareness of and reference to flow in popular media is growing. Increasingly, I am finding that I don't need to explain what flow is when sharing the main focus of my work in psychology. I still need to pronounce Mike's surname, but now I hear people referring to flow as a familiar state. I think this is partly to do with the exponential rise of the information age, where access to ideas is readily available. Also, I think it is attributable to the increasing value people are placing on experience over materialism. And probably the most important reason for the growth in awareness about flow is its relevance to all walks of life.

Access to Descriptions of Flow in the Information Age

The information age we are living in provides unprecedented access to information, and as new technologies take on traction, ways of accessing information have diversified. From hard copy books to e-books, and from live interviews on TV to online podcasts, the convenience of gaining information has created a society where we can be well-informed and influenced by the latest knowledge in areas of personal interest. Podcasts have become the buzz activity of the last 10 years. While they were definitely on the rise pre-COVID, the number of people who purchased podcast mics over COVID was massive, and the podcast industry has thrived during and since the pandemic.[1]

As a keen listener of health and wellness podcasts, I take notice when I hear the experience of flow being referred to, and I hear such references more frequently. I'll share a few examples. On Peter Attia's popular podcast, *The Drive*, Oliver Burkeman was interviewed about insights from his book *Four Thousand Weeks*, which provides a thought-provoking perspective on time, productivity, and purpose. Burkeman addressed a question by Attia on the sense of meaning. Burkeman shared that in his experience, what makes the best times in life are either times we look back on fondly, or they are flow states:

> *In my experience, the best times in life are either the best in recollection, in hindsight, or they are flow states. With flow states, can you be aware that you are in them? I think, in some bodily sense you can be aware you are in them. But you're not in them once you're thinking about them in a verbal way.²*

Burkeman pointed out how flow can be attained—and then quickly lost if you start to reflect on being in the experience while in it. This is because you've moved from total absorption in what you were doing to entertaining a cognition about it, such as how good it feels to be in flow or how everything is going so well. Evaluation enters, and flow disappears.

Another interviewee on Peter Attia's *The Drive* podcast, Mark Messier, who played at the top level in the NHL hockey league for 25 years, also spoke eloquently about the many factors that come together at the same time for flow/peak performance to be experienced:

> *I think it is a level of concentration that often doesn't get discovered. It is a deep level of concentration that you are not even aware of. That is mixed with preparation. That is mixed with belief. That is mixed with repetition of the skill. All of that comes together at a certain time.³*

Sam Kerr, captain of the Australian women's soccer team, the Matildas, spoke about the essence of flow (albeit without using the term) in a press conference prior to the start of the 2023 Women's World Cup held in Australia:

> *We have to just live in the moment. We spoke about it briefly today. It's okay to feel nervous or okay to get overshadowed by the crowd because that's life, that's football. We can talk about it, but it's about being in the moment and supporting one another.*

Kerr is regarded as the leading women's striker in the game, and her calm composure on and off the field illustrates her skill of being in the present moment, recognizing nervousness, and letting it go to focus in the moment.

In a 2024 podcast interview hosted by Michael Gervais, 5-time Olympic medalist in the sport of women's artistic gymnastics, Nastia Liukin responded to a final question by performance psychologist Gervais about what she might want to wish for the gymnasts preparing to compete in the Paris Olympics. Without hesitation, Liukin replied, *"Be present."* She recounted that during her gold-medal-winning Olympic all-around performance in the 2008 Beijing Games, she spent much of her time outside of competing not being present but instead constantly thinking about what was next. Illustrating how important one's quality of experience is, Liukin shared, *"The importance of just being present and grateful is so much stronger than the feeling of the outcome."*[4]

Being in the moment is one of the many inspiring things one of the greatest basketballers to take the court, Michael Jordan, has talked about. In the acclaimed ESPN docuseries *The Last Dance*, I recall Jordan saying, *"Live in the moment, for the moment."* The Last Dance followed the Chicago Bulls in their 1997-98 season and their quest for a sixth NBA title. Sportswriter Mark Vancil, who has written extensively about Michael Jordan, described him in an interview in *The Last Dance* in the following way:

> *Michael was a mystic; he was never anywhere else.*
> *His gift was not that he could jump higher, run faster,*
> *or shoot a basketball. His gift was that he was*
> *completely present, and that was the separator.*[5]

This quote by Vancil is interesting, as, without a doubt, Jordan *could* jump higher, run faster, and shoot a basketball better than most of his peers. Vancil, who had spent many hours observing and talking with

Jordan, perceived his main gift was, however, his ability to be completely present; that is, to be in flow.

Moving from sport to creative expression in the arts, we can also observe flow as a motivator of experience. In fact, it was through studying painters that Mike Csikszentmihalyi first examined flow in his doctoral thesis on creativity. A contemporary painter, Leslie Tejada, wrote that her creative process "*. . . has been learning to let go. Trusting in the creative flow, I have gradually learned to paint from the inside-out.*"[6] Tejada shared that she would clear her mind by going for a walk and "*that it is in the clear space of a quiet mind that ideas and inspirations emerge.*"

Writer and well-known film critic Roger Ebert wrote about dropping into the zone, a term often popularly used to describe flow, when he worked:

> *When I write, I fall into the zone many writers, painters, musicians, athletes, and craftsmen of all sorts seem to share: In doing something I enjoy and am an expert at, deliberate thought falls aside, and it is all just THERE. I think of the next word no more than the composer thinks of the next note.*[7]

Ebert illustrated how flow isn't something one can reach by striving for it. Instead, there is a certain level of trust that flow may arise, once one has experienced it and so knows what the state is at an experiential level. This experience where words effortlessly follow words, or the next action seamlessly arises from the one preceding, is one of the most enjoyable aspects of being in flow. Where one's usual experience may involve effort and a sense of working hard at something, when touching flow, there is ease and effortless rhythm. In flow, we also experience a performance level that creates work that is satisfying and motivates us to return to this state again.

Creative pursuits of all types lend themselves to flow. This comment came from actress Taylor Schilling,

> *Life is so much easier when I allow myself to BE myself and go with the flow, whatever that looks like on a given day. If I can get quiet enough to truly check in with myself, I usually end up on the right track.*[8]

Another actor, Willem Dafoe, in an interview about his work, referred to qualities of flow as motivators for what drives him both in screen and in stage roles. Referring to the feeling of being engrossed in a part, Dafoe said:

> *Sometimes, when you're performing, the world drops away, and you have a sort of awakening. I try to seek out that experience, and that's what keeps me going, I guess. It's being engaged in a full way.*[9]

Interestingly, the highly successful Dafoe has been a long-term student of yoga and meditation, which he credits with helping him to cultivate concentration and equanimity.[10]

Surgeons were one of the first groups to be interviewed by Mike when he was developing his flow framework. My colleague and long-term meditation proponent, John Hendry, recently shared with me an encounter he had with one of his ex-students from Geelong Grammar School. This student, who was introduced to flow through John's work at Geelong Grammar, went on to become an open-heart surgeon. During my interview with John, he shared having been at lunch with this surgeon the previous week. They were talking about being in flow, and the surgeon shared a story about a challenging procedure he had in front of him the next day.

The patient he was to perform open heart surgery on was not able to accept blood transfusions, and the surgeon shared with John that it would be important for him to be totally in flow during the procedure. He said it was so important because of decisions he had to make that, if he were over-analyzing, fear would creep in, and he couldn't allow that. Instead, he had to remain acutely focused. The surgeon also explained that he could detect fear within his team when he was discussing the upcoming difficult procedure with them, and that this strengthened his resolve that in the procedure, fear could not be permitted. Instead, he focused on trusting his skills and encouraged his team to do the same. John touched base with the surgeon the evening following the procedure, where the surgeon recounted how everything, including time, just disappeared during the surgery. He was just working, and everyone on the team was fully engaged, just as he was. After the operation, he thanked everyone working with him, and he reflected on how the whole team seemed to be in flow during the procedure. The medical team was able to turn their fear into trust and to focus fully on the challenge of the operation.

It is very satisfying to see growth in awareness of flow state through examples such as this of describing flow in their work. I look forward to the continued development of flow research and the continuation of a growing conversation about flow in the popular media. Equally important to me is maintaining Mike's conceptualization of flow, and this has been a prime motivator in writing this book—to set out the flow experience as taught to me by Csikszentmihalyi. There are people promoting flow across different domains, which, in general, is good to see. What can be disappointing is when flow is rebranded into an experience that is different from how Mike conceptualized the experience. From personal conversations with Mike and with those who had worked closely with him for many years, I am aware that he was not in favor of approaches that focused on over-sensationalizing the concept or using flow as a vehicle to advance one's own agenda in a related area. However, Mike was the consummate European gentleman and refrained from talking in public about his perceptions of research or popular press that were questionable in terms of advancing an authentic understanding of flow.

What Flow is Not

Recognizing what is *not* flow state is important to clearly understand what the flow experience is.

One use of the word flow was definitely not what Csikszentmihalyi intended when he chose this term. The use of the phrase "go with the flow" often connotes a laissez-faire, passive approach that is not the purposeful, focused flow state described by Csikszentmihalyi. The "roll with the punches" and take things as they come approach, often denoted by the phrase "go with the flow," is definitely not Mike's concept of flow, which is an active and engaged psychological state.

Flow is not the exclusive purview of extreme sport athletes, although extreme sport athletes do undoubtedly encounter flow in what they do. However, flow is theoretically accessible to all. By definition, anyone who can perceive the level of challenge in a situation, understand the level of skill they possess, and have the ability to modify one or both conditions has the potential to experience flow.

Flow is not peak performance, although the latter does often occur when in flow. Peak performance refers to an outcome or achievement of superior functioning rather than to an internal experience of optimal feelings and perceptions. Flow describes an inner psychological state while engaged in an effortful and challenging activity, whereas peak performance refers to the outcome or accomplishment as a consequence of sustained effort and concentration. It is possible to achieve peak performance without the accompanying state of flow. Sometimes, it is possible to achieve something at a higher level than one has previously achieved by sheer grit or welcome luck. It is important to remember that flow is a psychological state, an inner experience. And Mike was much more interested in the quality of experience we encounter in life than the achievements that flow leads to, especially if we achieve a goal without paying attention to the quality of experience along the way. As Mike wrote,

> *As soon as the emphasis shifts from the experience per se to what you can accomplish with it, we are back in the realm of everyday life ruled by extrinsic considerations.*[11]

Flow might involve a peak experience, which Maslow defined as moments of highest happiness. Peak experience moments are those moments that we remember as the most memorable in our lives. However, flow and peak experiences may occur independently of each other. Peak experiences often involve flow, but flow can occur without it being a peak experience. Further, flow involves not just an emotional experience but several important cognitive components, including total concentration, clear goals, and perceptions of a balance between challenges and skills.

There's an aspect of flow described by Mike that further demonstrates that flow and peak experience may be different. That is the idea that there are levels of flow, which Mike referred to as micro and macro flow. While *macro flow* experiences might well resemble peak experiences, flow can occur in daily activities, such as housework or reading a book. Calling such daily encounters with positive subjective experience *microflow*, Mike explained that these low-level flow experiences, over time, can have a big influence on the quality of our lives and are thus important to be aware of. Mike wrote an entire book about daily flow experiences called *Finding Flow: The Psychology of Engagement with Everyday Life*.

Why Flow Makes Life Worth Living

Flow is the experience that makes life worth living, and it is a key motivation for us to continue our involvement in a flow-producing activity. From my interview with Simon, a professional road cyclist, comes a clear illustration of how flow can become the reason for continued engagement in an activity:

> *There's nothing, there's no experience in sport that is as exhilarating or rewarding as being in flow. That's what makes me keep riding, knowing I might get it again.*

For a psychological state to become the raison d'etre of engaging in an activity speaks to its value. This is the value of flow I've heard time and time again when discussing the state with people from all walks of life. Expanding research that furthers Mike's seminal contributions will lead to a better understanding of what is happening when we are in flow, how we can tap into this special state, and, most important, why it matters that we do.

I found in Johann Hari's excellent book *Stolen Focus: Why You Can't Pay Attention* a simple yet profound description of the difference experiencing flow can make to our lives. Internationally bestselling author Hari interviewed many leaders in their respective fields in researching his book on the factors contributing to a decrease in ability to sustain attention throughout society today. One of these people was Mike Csikszentmihalyi, toward the end of his life. Hari recounts how his interview with Mike and learning about the state of effortless focus that flow is, helped him to see that we all have an important choice to make:

> *I felt in that moment that we all have a choice now between two profound forces—fragmentation or flow. Fragmentation makes you smaller, shallower, angrier. Flow makes you bigger, deeper, calmer. Fragmentation shrinks us. Flow expands us.*[12]

How does flow lead to such a pivotal impact? Mike has explained that flow is important for two main reasons. First, for the immediate quality of experience it provides. The second reason is related to growth. Mike described how flow leads to personal growth through the coming together of two processes: differentiation and integration.[13] Differentiation refers to becoming more uniquely yourself. Integration refers to connection with others and with new ideas and insights. Mike argued that flow experiences lead to greater complexity within the self through these processes of differentiation and integration. In this way, flow allows us to grow, both as an individual, and as a person able to make valued contributions to society. Mike summed up these ideas about why flow is important in the following statement:

> *Flow is important both because it makes the present instant more enjoyable and because it builds the self-confidence that allows us to develop skills and make significant contributions to humankind.*[14]

This statement by Mike about why flow is important illustrates how flow experiences can create a more enjoyable and meaningful life through the development of skills and the subsequent making of significant contributions to society. This became an important focus for Mike's later work, exemplified in his books that followed his popular 1990 book, *Flow*. In 1994, Mike published *The Evolving Self: A Psychology for the Third Millennium*, where he sets out in detail his ideas about developing complexity in consciousness. Then, in 1996, in *Creativity: Flow and The Psychology of Discovery and Invention*, Mike writes about his in-depth interviews with creative achievers who exemplify living lives in flow.

Mike's work was about making a positive impact on the quality of life experiences people could work toward. Once we know about flow experience and how to facilitate flow in our lives, we can also choose to direct our energies toward making positive contributions by learning to harness our psychological energy toward meaningful tasks and goals.

If we don't harness our psychological energy in a purposeful way, we risk experiencing negative states of consciousness. In the flow models described earlier in the book, apathy is the opposite experience to flow and is a very negative state to be in. Apathy is defined by the absence of challenge and skill. Just like flow is important both for its immediate experience and for what it can allow one to contribute in the longer term, so apathy is recognized not just for the immediate experience it provides but also for its potentially detrimental long-term effects on motivation and cognition.

Recent research has indicated that apathy is problematic in the long term and is associated with cognitive decline. In a large-scale, prospective longitudinal study, cognitive decline at age 74 was not associated with having had an active job, defined by the study authors as involving high demands and high control.[15] Rather, it was associated with having a passive job (defined as low demands and low control) throughout one's life. The experiential dimension of apathy, as depicted in the eight-channel model, is one of low (or no) demand and is often associated with a feeling of being stuck or unable to change one's situation. Thus, the long-term experience of apathy may have a deleterious impact on cognitive function, as well as on motivation to act.

Finding that a passive job leads to a faster cognitive decline with age is an important finding to reflect on if you want to optimize your cognitive abilities as you age. Interestingly, the same study found that being in a high-strain job, defined as one involving high demands and low control, was also associated with cognitive decline. This type of job situation would be similar to the experiences of worry and anxiety in the eight-channel flow model. So, just as with apathy, experiencing anxiety without the skill or means to change the perceived negative characteristics of this state may, over the long term, be associated with poor cognitive outcomes.

Flow occurs beyond the negative experiences of boredom or apathy, and beyond those of worry or anxiety. Flow is not just enjoyable; it contributes to our growth in complexity. With so much that flow can offer us, my hope is that this book can contribute to increasing awareness about this special state and how it can contribute to a life well-lived.

CHAPTER 11

Experience Matters

It is useful to remember occasionally that life unfolds as a chain of subjective experiences...The quality of these experiences determines whether, and to what extent life was worth living.[1]

—Csikszentmihalyi

Life is a Chain of Subjective Experiences

Throughout this book, I have drawn distinctions between performance and experience and argued that the latter deserves more attention in our lives. Whether we are an elite level performer or someone going about a regular, non-high-performance life, recognizing how important quality of experience is matters a lot. Pursuing mastery, working on mindfulness skills, and being open to the experience of flow can make for a rich life. Hazel shared her thoughts on living a life like this, reinforcing my argument that these concepts are not just for high-performing individuals but instead are relevant and valuable for everyone:

> *I think it might be easy for people to go like, "Oh, well, that's just for elite-level athletes," or like, "That's just for people who care about performance." But I really think that if more people understood these concepts and valued them, we'd probably have a slightly different society. Flow, mastery, mindfulness—they're actually more meaningful, more valuable, more important than you might think.*

As a performance psychologist, I work with high-functioning individuals, training psychological skills to help them navigate the chosen challenges they have decided to pursue. Many of these individuals are on a path of extraordinary achievement, bringing their innate gifts and talents to a challenge that also demands extreme effort and long-standing perseverance. A challenge that provides no assured outcomes. Whether it be through injury, selection policies, or plain bad luck, many well-deserving high performers fail to reach their ultimate pinnacle of achievement. Or, they have to face failure many times along their path, a path that may or may not lead to eventual success. In this way, the elite performers of the world are not so dissimilar from the rest of us.

Each of us brings to our own life challenges the best of ourselves. We are not guaranteed any successful outcome and may encounter much difficulty in life. The uncertainty of our lives and the uncertainty of the fulfillment of our dreams means that the experience we encounter along the journey becomes a key marker of our life satisfaction.

It was only through in-depth reading of Mike's books and conversations with him about the value of flow that I came to recognize why it is *experience* that really matters. I recognized that what I initially saw as a psychological state to optimize performance was, in fact, equally, or actually *more* about the quality of experience that flow provided. This lesson was first brought home to me, as I have mentioned, when I began interviewing elite athletes about their flow experiences. The gratefulness expressed by these athletes—for the opportunity to talk in-depth about how flow made their sport experiences memorable—was striking. To have participants thank me, the researcher, for giving them the opportunity to talk about their optimal experiences is something I will never forget. It helped me to understand first-hand what Mike was writing about almost ten years earlier—about the critical importance of the quality of experience we encounter in life. How life unfolds as a chain of subjective experiences, and how these experiences influence the life we get to live.

In *Flow in Sports,* Mike and I wrote about how, even though we *play* sport, we don't *work* sport; it can become just another serious activity we take part in.[2] Certainly, for professional athletes, sport is their work. However, most people who take part in sport are not professional athletes. And those who are professional athletes likely have begun taking part in their sport for enjoyment, but in many cases, could benefit from re-connecting with the factors that intrinsically motivated them about their sport. As MJ so famously said, it's about playing for the "love of the game."

Jordan's motivation to take part in the activity he loved, for the experience it gave him, illustrates what Mike referred to as an autotelic personality. Can you think of people in your life who demonstrate intrinsic motivation toward an activity they engage in regularly, be that sport, work, or involvement in the arts? Perhaps this describes your own life? Would you dedicate much of your time and energy toward your performance work, regardless of whether you were paid or received some other external incentive for your involvement? Do you find in your main activity autotelic experiences?

Learning to be Autotelic

The autotelic experience, as defined in Chapter 3 on the dimensions of flow, is an intrinsically rewarding experience. When we do something for the enjoyment it gives, with no expectation or need for other outcomes, we are intrinsically motivated toward that activity. If we find several of the activities that we engage in to be intrinsically motivating, and we find flow in these engagements, there's a good chance we have an autotelic personality.

Hazel, who you have come to know about through her experiences shared throughout sections of this book, is a classic example of an autotelic individual. This was evident to me when I first got to know her, and her stories have been interspersed throughout the chapters on anxiety, mastery, and mindfulness. At the end of our interview, I asked Hazel what motivates her to climb. Her immediate response described beautifully what an "autotelic" experience feels like, and the positive impact flow can have on one's life:

> *I mean, you know this is a very simple answer—it is flow. I think that's really the main thing, honestly. If I have flow experience, I'll just be happier for the next few days. I'll be much happier. So, it just really supports my well-being. That's the main reason I climb. I've got more energy. I feel lighter. I feel more hopeful and positive about my life. And what's coming.*

I've heard from many people I've interviewed over the years this idea that flow becomes the over-arching reason for participating in their activity or performance domain. Once experienced, flow motivates us to experience this special state again. It is because of the positive potential for flow to contribute to a rich and meaningful life that I have written this book so that more people can appreciate the value of flow in their lives. But is flow something we only experience when life is going well?

What About the Experience of Adversity?

A researcher of flow, Richard Logan, used the term "the people of flow" to describe the individuals he studied who were able to turn difficult situations into flow experiences.[3] Not just any old difficult situation—Logan examined the experiences of people who endured extreme physical ordeals, such as polar explorers and prisoners of concentration camps. Logan argued that surviving such trying circumstances involved these individuals aligning their attention toward aspects they could focus on and control.

For example, Logan recounted how prisoners of war would come up with mathematical calculations related to the size of their cell, or the length of time in minutes they expected to spend locked up in a confined space. One such prisoner described making a thread from a towel into a quasi-tape measure, which he then set about using to measure everything in his cell. Individuals facing terrifying ordeals have overwhelming demands, such that their challenge levels are off the chart. In order for the challenge-skill balance of flow to occur at all, they need to find a way to limit the stimulus field and focus their attention on something they have some control over, which allows them to get absorbed in the activity. Logan also suggested that these *people of flow* are inherently skilled at not getting caught up in themselves. Remembering that loss of self-consciousness is a dimension of flow, Logan argued that people in the midst of horrible ordeals who are able to find flow have a better-than-average capacity to not dwell on themselves. Mike wrote about these people of flow in several of his books and argued that the ability to drop self-consciousness was integral to an autotelic person.

> *With enough psychic energy free to observe and analyze their surroundings objectively, they have a better chance of discovering in them new opportunities for action. If we were to consider one trait a key element of the autotelic personality, this might be it.*[4]

By not getting caught up in themselves, autotelic individuals are more in tune with what is happening around them, including opportunities to find flow.

Adversity can thus be thought of as another opportunity to find flow. In adversity, we can still choose to focus attention on a task over which we can exert some control and invest attention fully in this space. And by so doing, we can maintain some personal control in situations where external factors are the dominating force at play.

Even in adversity, what we choose to focus on defines the experience we encounter. We can be free of suffering or experience a life of suffering. In either case, we do have a choice of what to focus our attention on. A great historical example of this is the Auschwitz survivor Viktor Frankl.

Frankl did not just survive Auschwitz; he found meaning in the life he was forced into by using his skill as a medical doctor to help other prisoners. He also shared his indomitable spirit, first with his fellow prisoners and years later, once the war was over, in publishing his dramatically inspiring book, *Man's Search for Meaning* (1946).

Frankl, as a young Austrian psychiatrist, had been developing a theory of psychotherapy and was writing a book about his theory at the time of being imprisoned. His nearly complete manuscript, its pages hidden inside his coat, was taken from him when he entered his first concentration camp. Can you imagine if the only copy of the book you'd spent many months and perhaps years writing was taken from you and there was no backup? Frankl was undeterred. He visualized his manuscript, and in his head, he wrote it over and over, as well as on any tiny bits of paper he could find, during his three years in concentration camps. In so doing, he found purpose, focus, and hope. Upon his release from being a prisoner of war, Frankl wrote and published his book, describing how he survived—and how we all can identify a purpose in life, imagine it, live it. When we consider what his circumstances were, this awe-inspiring quote from Frankl reminds us of our ultimate freedom as human beings:

> *Everything can be taken from a man, but one thing:*
> *the last of the human freedoms—to choose one's*
> *attitude in any given set of circumstances, to choose*
> *one's own way.*[5]

Most of us are fortunate to have many more freedoms than Frankl experienced as a prisoner of war. Life in the 21st century offers more opportunities than in previous generations. For many of us, the things we worry about are not matters of life or death. Yet, still, we worry and wish we were someone else or someplace else. Frankl's story might help us to shift our perspective from what we don't have to the freedoms we do have. Including the one freedom Frankl relied on to stay alive when most around him were dying—the freedom to choose what to focus on.

What we choose to focus on largely determines the quality of our experience as we travel through life. Viktor Frankl is an extraordinary example of doing so. We can look around the microcosm of the society we operate within and find examples of people who are choosing not to focus on their adversity but rather on the potential opportunity adversity has handed them. And we no doubt see others who are unable to pick themselves up after life deals them an unlucky and difficult hand. This is not to deny that there is inequity in the world and that some are better positioned than others to thrive in the face of difficult circumstances based on their demographic. However, there is within inescapable suffering a window of freedom, even if it is small, by recognizing that we always have the power to choose where to focus our attention.

Take 2—A Personal Reminder of the Importance of Finding Meaning in Adversity

> *When something bad happens, you have three choices.*
> *You can either let it define you, let it destroy you, or*
> *you can let it strengthen you.*
>
> —Dr. Suess

It is easier to write about the amazing attitudes of people such as Viktor Frankl than to embody their perspective. It is easy to get caught up in our personal suffering and not find the opportunities it provides for learning and growth. I learned this lesson again just recently. A year of celebrating my 60th birthday in 2023 ended badly; definitely not in the way I had anticipated. I had enjoyed two amazing trips to beautiful parts of Australia over the course of that year. The first, to the Kimberley Coast, was an eye-opening experience. The majesty, the untouched physical beauty of this section of the West Australian coastline, seen from a small charter boat and helicopter, gave me many unforgettable experiences. So did the amazingly clear waters and coral life of the coral cay of Lady Elliott Island in the southern Great Barrier Reef. These experiences gave me a strong appreciation for the natural beauty of Australia.

In mid-December, I ventured to Fiji with my two adult sons for what was to be my final celebration for my 60th birthday. We had a fun time and got immersed in the local Fijian culture. Then, two days before the end of our trip, I woke up with a swollen underside of my right foot. Having no idea what caused it, I wasn't sure how to manage it. I became less and less sure as the skin on the front of my big toe also became red and swollen. The pain was intense, and one of the hardest days I've had to endure physically was the all-day travel back from the small, remote island of Fiji we were staying on to Brisbane.

Christmas in hospital

Upon arriving back in Brisbane, it was straight to Emergency. It was Christmas Eve, relatively quiet in the Emergency Center of the private hospital I went to, and I figured I might have to stay for a few hours of IV antibiotics. The infectious disease specialist who took over my case told me I had to be admitted, and soon I was lying in a hospital room, hooked up to potent IV antibiotics, and contemplating Christmas Day in the hospital. This was definitely not part of my plan. I woke on Christmas morning feeling horribly unwell, and the days to follow were the same. Besides the pain of the foot, lying in a hospital bed did my back no favors, and I was in discomfort from that, too. My sleep tracker told me that I averaged 2-3 hours of sleep a night for 11 consecutive nights. When I usually operate on a minimum of 6 and preferably 7-8 hours/night, having such poor sleep was terrible for my immunity. I began fighting a viral infection I caught in the hospital ward, as well as fighting the serious bacterial infection I acquired in Fiji. I tried explaining to the night shift nurses that waking me every 4 hours to take observations was not helping my immunity, as I had a big infection to fight. That argument landed on deaf ears. Hospitals, I soon learned, work on set procedures, and there's no room for individual experiences.

I made little progress, and after several days on IV antibiotics, I was sent for an MRI, which revealed a large abscess within the infected area and explained the minimal effect of the antibiotics at that time. Then, it was a waiting game for emergency surgery. Three days later, a kind orthopedic and trauma surgeon created an emergency list for me. New Year's Day 2024 began somewhat differently from what I'd planned.

Surgery, I was told, went well, and a couple of days later, I was able to be discharged, along with a stash of oral antibiotics. It was good to be home, back with my two cats who had missed me greatly, and to the comfort of my own bed. But I quickly learned that 12 days of lying in a hospital bed leads to a huge loss of muscle strength, and most of my energy was still being directed toward healing my foot. I was on crutches and learned the challenge of navigating my stairs. I made a mental note to myself to choose single-level living next time I move!

Unwanted Challenges

I am not averse to taking medication, but that stops with antibiotics. I had experienced a very bad reaction to antibiotics in the mid-90s, which left my digestive system overly sensitive. Since that time, I have stringently avoided antibiotics unless they were absolutely necessary. I understood this was one of those situations and that I had to put up with digestive upset that worsened the more days I was on killer antibiotics. I was reaching that fine line of antibiotics starting to do more harm than good. Then, at one point, the tables were definitely turned toward the more harmful effects. I learned after being home from the hospital for a week that I had developed from all the antibiotics in the hospital a bacterial overgrowth that required eradication—with, guess what, different antibiotics! This was close to a breaking point for me. Having to take more antibiotics and experience their side effects was an unwelcome experience. But doing nothing and risking a more severe illness was not an option.

Another unwelcome challenge was learning to live for an extended period without daily workouts. Before the accident, being active was an everyday routine, and if I did miss a day of exercise, I felt lower in energy and mood. Now I looked at my muscle mass literally withering away before my eyes, and I realized I had spent 12 days without seeing the sunlight or smelling the fresh air. And while I could now go out into my courtyard to catch some morning sunlight, there was no exercise happening for several weeks. My energy was still being directed at healing my foot, which was morphing every day into a new visual eyesore as the infected skin started cracking away, bringing a pain experience different from the ones that had come before.

I was aware that there are always lessons to be learned from stressful and negative life experiences. But I felt for some weeks with this foot injury that there was nothing positive to take from what was happening to me. That it was just damn bad luck—which my medical team told me it was. There was never an identifiable cause for my getting a staph infection and abscess. All the treating doctors told me I was extremely unlucky. The fact that there wasn't an identifiable event, not even a visible cut or abrasion to the area that became infected, reinforced even more a sense of being *really* unlucky. I'd spent most of 2023 rebuilding from various musculoskeletal injuries to have my health and fitness lost with a random but serious infection. Having no celebrations over Christmas and New Year, but instead lying in an uncomfortable hospital bed, undoing all the good work I'd put into my physical health seemed just plain unfair.

During this time of challenge that I faced, I did not cope as well as the people facing adversity Richard Logan wrote about. People who faced far more grueling challenges than my own. People who found purpose in the most extreme of situations by limiting their attention to what they could control. By finding ways to create challenge-skill balance in their immediate environments, these people from Logan's research were able to turn difficult situations into flow experiences.

My challenge-skill balance ratio had me sitting most of the time in the anxiety channel due to the lack of a clear diagnosis, and the concomitant uncertainty over the prognosis. When not experiencing anxiety, I was bored due to not being able to do anything productive for the almost two weeks I was in hospital. I did look for ways to create a challenge-skill balance by delimiting my focus to the challenges present in each new day that I did have a margin of control over. I set tiny goals, as these were the only ones I could set—like what to order for the next day's meals from the hospital's extensive but mostly unpalatable menu. Or when to try moving from my hospital bed to the adjacent chair, and in my latter days in hospital, venturing out of my room into the hallways on crutches or in a wheelchair. I did not have control over much during this time, but I did seek out small ways in which to make each day more bearable. I found in reading, listening to audio books, (and watching Netflix) that I could control my focus to areas outside the uncontrollable challenge I was facing with the injury. When I did manage my internal world, I found much more peace and much less anxiety than when I let the injury challenge overwhelm me. The uncontrollables remained but by focusing on not getting caught up in them, but rather on whatever aspects I could control, I created a much more positive immediate environment in which to operate. I wish I could say I found flow, but I think most of the time, I was wavering between anxiety and boredom.

The power of feedback

I received two sources of input at this time of coming close to drowning in self-pity. One came from one of my doctors who had worked in tropical areas and said he'd seen such infections lead to amputations. That was a sobering thought. The second input was from George Mumford, who sent me good wishes for the new year. I wrote back to let him know I was in the hospital and outlined what had happened. George sent back a message of best wishes for my recovery. Then I received a follow-up message from George that I straight away balked at:

"No Struggle No Swag. I am just saying."

"Yes, George," I wrote back. "It is a great saying, but when the swag is not one that I want, i.e., this injury, infection, and pain, wondering how it applies??"

George wrote back:

You get to choose the attitude you have toward unavoidable suffering. What's the lesson?

Viktor Frankl said when you find meaning in suffering it ceases to be suffering. Something happens and we get to interpret it in a way that empowers, inspires, moves us. Kobe Bryant, my sister, and my best friend from high school died in a period of one week. I interpreted it in a way that empowered me. For example, I interpreted Kobe's death this way: he's had a positive impact on so many people in death, more than he could have had if he lived 100 years.

I humbly thanked George and told him I was going to think about what he'd written and find meaning somehow. George wrote again, telling me: *"You are an amazing woman, and you can do anything you set your mind to do. You are a Masterpiece!"*

I thanked George for how his words helped me, and it was a reminder of how George's work and attitude have helped so many people. Find the meaning in suffering, George wrote to me. Remember what you've read from Viktor Frankl, he reminded me. Suffering ceases to be suffering when meaning can be found in it. Although I struggled to find meaning in the midst of the pain and restrictions associated with the injury, I can look back now and see that I have come out the other end stronger. And perhaps a bit wiser.

Learnings

A couple of initial learning experiences from the injury that stood out for me had to do with the pace at which I usually live my life, and how you learn a lot about people when in a time of need. The first lesson came when the pace at which I usually lived came to an abrupt halt once I entered the hospital. I never lie down other than to sleep, and to find myself hooked up to an IV and feeling so unwell, unable to get out of my hospital bed, took all my joie de vivre away. It felt like a balloon had been popped inside of me that instantly took from me all my energy, enjoyment, and sense of purpose. All the time doing very little did, however, cause me to reflect on the busyness of my life and whether building in some downtime going forward might be beneficial—perhaps even enjoyable.

Returning home from the hospital meant I had to move more, as no longer were there nurses on call, and I had two flights of stairs to navigate on crutches. Plus, if I wanted to eat, I had to forage something up with one free hand; I had to use the other to balance on my one good leg. I found these basic everyday tasks exhausting, and I even wondered whether it might have been better to stay in the hospital a bit longer. After sleeping through the night in my own bed, I soon lost that thought.

Even though I was up and about more than when in the hospital, my activity options were very confined. I missed being physically active and the positive energy I found from my usual daily workouts. I wasn't able to drive, and I became reliant on the kindness of others to get me to appointments and pick up groceries for me.

This is where the second lesson kicked in—seeing how the various people in my life responded in this time of heightened need I had for assistance. When I let people know about my injury, most were shocked to hear what I'd experienced, and everyone expressed their good wishes. Some also made it clear that they were too busy to lend a hand. This hit hard initially, as I really needed support, and I rarely ask for outside assistance. To put it out there that I was looking for help and have it come back to me unrecognized or ignored was a tough lesson.

Other people I encountered during this time stood out for how much help they were willing to provide. One person who helped get me through this time was a friend who had been dropping in to say hello to my cats while I was in the hospital. I asked Alina whether she might have any time to stop by once I was home, and not only did she do so, but she also took it upon herself to ensure I had food and to help me with the tasks I couldn't do by myself. I had at the time been enquiring with home help organizations the hospital had recommended to me after leaving their line of 24/7 assistance, and I decided to ask Alina if she'd be interested in being my hired home help. I liked the idea of having someone who knew me and whom I trusted to a stranger in my home. Alina agreed and provided wonderful support over the next few weeks as I started to learn how to walk on my injured foot again while dealing with gut issues post-antibiotics.

There were other friends who made time to stop by, and these visits provided opportunities to reconnect, which otherwise busy lives generally prevented from occurring. Then there was the kindness of strangers. Steve, the husband of my cleaner, Lenie, whom I employed on a more frequent basis during this time of immobility, picked up his wife after a morning of cleaning and dropped off for me a huge shepherd's pie and chicken casserole. I'd never met Steve, and here he was, spending his Saturday cooking up meals for someone he didn't know. When I thanked Steve, he said that I'd been going through such a tough time, and he hoped the meals would be a small help. They were, and more so, this gesture of kindness and generosity will remain with me. Steve and Lenie returned with a second large home-cooked meal the following week.

I experienced other examples of people in my life reaching out, whether it was an offer to pick up groceries, or dropping off a meal, or flowers. Witnessing the kindness of people was heartening at this time. It also helped to offset the disappointment I felt regarding the few people whom I thought were my friends dropping off the radar once expressing their regrets at what I was going through. I was listening to an audio book called *How We Break* by health psychologist Vincent Deary at the time of recuperating from my injury. In his book, Deary writes about research on responses to stress and trauma with real-life case studies of people facing difficult circumstances. Deary shares how one of the most bitter learnings of living through a difficult time is finding out who will be there for you:

> *If you want to know who your friends really are, have a prolonged crisis. After a couple of months, you might be surprised at how few are left standing.*[6]

Having experienced relative isolation at the time of my injury, I have been reminded of the importance of being present and connected enough to recognize when a friend is in need and offering support at such times if it is possible to do so. I've also been reminded that other people in (or out) of our lives are not a controllable aspect of our experience and that the impact of others has the potential to either help us move forward—or to be an obstacle to our progress. When we think about what helps or hinders us from experiencing flow in a particular life domain or situation, recognizing the role of the people we interact with is a factor to consider.

As I found when interviewing team sport athletes, the people immediately around you can either help or hinder you from finding flow. Athletes spoke to me about how when the team was playing well and communicating positively with each other, flow was facilitated. Conversely, when the team was either not performing well, or there were negative interactions between players or between players and other people in their environment, flow was hindered. The presence of other people in your life or performance domain makes for another, mostly uncontrollable factor in your quest for flow.

Since, for many of us, the domains we operate in do tend to involve other people, recognizing that the quality of the interactions we have is a powerful force to either help, or hinder, our experience of flow, is definitely worth taking into consideration. My friend and colleague, John Hendry, emphasized in our conversations around this book his perspective that flow is ultimately relational. John shared with me his perspective that for flow to be experienced, "*. . . one needs to be at peace with oneself and be at peace with the relational context encountered. This 'at peace' tempers anxiety, makes it work for you, and enables you to fully engage.*"

Learning to Live with the Uncontrollables

As I reflect on my experience during the time of this injury, I can see that there was, in the first few weeks, a lack of peace with myself, and a lack of peace with the relational context I encountered, particularly during my time in hospital, and immediately after. In retrospect, I can see that I got too caught up in what I could not control, and this pulled me into an initially mostly downward quality of experience trajectory.

There are, of course, many uncontrollable factors as we navigate our life challenges. Frankl's life experience is a classic example of this and of how it is possible to find meaning in times of extreme challenge and deprivation. I experienced my unwanted injury as a path of steps forward and backward. But I did come to realize there's a path. I came across an anonymous quote while navigating toward finding meaning in my unwanted challenge; it reminded me why I remained resolute on not giving in to my injury. I was walking out of my gym soon after starting back working out after my injury when I noticed a small quote attached to the gym exit door:

You either quit or keep going. They both hurt.

Sometimes, things seem so difficult that one feels like giving in, giving up, or stopping. But that, of course, leads to its own set of problems. Keeping going isn't an easy path—it hurts too—but there's at least some chance of success by choosing this path. As well, there's the possibility of finding flow—by matching the challenge you are facing with relevant skills, controlling the factors you can control, recognizing the factors you can't control that have the potential to impact your experience, and perhaps most importantly of all, trusting in the resilience of the human spirit. The famous quote by Nietzsche, *"What doesn't kill me makes me stronger,"* reminds us that suffering provides an opportunity to build strength and keep moving forward. If we can get out of our own way during a period of suffering and instead focus on where we have the potential to act, setting clear goals in a way that demarcates the challenges we have control over, flow may be on the horizon. And even if flow is not possible, perhaps not when we are right in the middle of adversity, we may at least find ways to curb a growing anxiety that is likely to occur when an ongoing challenge seems to outweigh our skills.

Embracing Experience to Grow

When we can learn to embrace experience, we have much more energy to focus on the present moment. While we are caught up in thinking about how we want things to be different, some of our attentional energy is devoted to what is wrong with the present situation and how we don't want it to be the way it is. We all have a finite level of attentional resources, and thus, the more we can focus on what is within our control in each present-moment situation in which we find ourselves, the more positive our quality of experience has the potential to be.

Remembering the three flow pre-conditions will help us move our experience toward the positive and toward flow. Setting clear goals and tuning into the feedback our environment is giving us helps to harness our attention and foster continued engagement in a deliberate and clear way. The other pre-condition is perhaps the most powerful of all: the relative balance between challenges and skills. Being open to challenging situations and then developing a skill set commensurate with the challenges sets the stage for flow. Over time, with a deliberate focus on defining the challenges and skills in your situation, you will become better at making the adjustments that will tip the scales closer to the high-challenge, high-skill equation that defines flow. Remember that both challenges and skills are tied in most closely with our perceptions, more than with any objective level of challenge or skill. And that when the challenge is high, recognizing the controllable challenges is crucial, along with an unshakeable trust in our skill set.

Through awareness of how the pre-conditions to flow express themselves in our own lives, we enhance our opportunity to experience this optimal state. Mike wrote that flow is important for two main reasons. First, for the experience it provides, the exhilarating moments of being fully connected to the present. The second reason is that growth in complexity is possible through flow experiences. This growth in complexity occurs through the processes of differentiation and integration. Once we have experienced flow in our lives, we value it for both these reasons. Initially, the focus is on the amazing experience of being in flow. Over time, as flow experiences accumulate, we come to understand ourselves better—both where we fit in with those around us and where we can identify ourselves as different and unique. As we encounter more instances of integration and differentiation, we become more able to understand how to contribute in significant ways to the world around us. And through having experienced flow, we develop self-confidence to take on challenging goals.

Learning to embrace the experience we are having brings us closer to flow. This is sometimes easy and sometimes difficult. When the stage is set for a flow experience, sometimes all that is required is to let things unfold and not get in our own way. At other times in life, the obstacles on our pathway can draw us into the experience of difficulty and suffering. Knowing that we can always choose where to focus our attention and that we can train our ability to come back to the present moment creates pathways to flow in many life situations.

Choosing to focus on the present—and not remaining at the mercy of our thoughts and feelings about situations we are facing—creates the space between stimulus and response. Learning that there is a pause between the in-breath and the out-breath, between what happens and how we respond to what happens—helps us to find the stillness within ourselves. This stillness is the jumping-off point for flow. You can cultivate stillness by training your mind to come to the present moment again and again. My wish is that through reading this book and developing the skills I've outlined that facilitate flow, you will find your stillness within and locate your own jumping-off point for optimal experience. And that by doing so, you will encounter many awe-inspiring flow experiences that contribute to a life well-lived.

Notes

Chapter 1

1. Mihaly Csikszentmihalyi, *Beyond boredom and anxiety*. (San Francisco: Jossey-Bass, 1975), 9.
2. Susan A. Jackson, "Athletes in flow: A qualitative investigation of flow states in elite figure skaters," *Journal of Applied Sport Psychology*, 4, no.2 (1992): 161-180, https://doi.org/10.1080/10413209208406459
3. Table 1 adapted, with permission, from Susan A. Jackson, "Factors influencing the occurrence of flow in elite athletes." *Journal of Applied Sport Psychology*, 7, no.2 (1995): 138-166, https://doi.org/10.1080/10413209508406962. Table adapted by permission from Informa UK Ltd, trading as Taylor & Francis Group.
4. Mihaly Csikszentmihalyi, "Toward a psychology of optimal experience." In L. Wheeler (Ed.), *Review of Personality and Social Psychology*, (Sage: Beverly Hills, 1982), 13.
5. Csikszentmihalyi, "Toward a psychology of optimal experience," 13.

Chapter 2

1. Sarah Steimer, "Mihaly "Mike" Csikszentmihalyi, pioneering psychologist, passes away at 87." *University of Chicago News*, Oct 27, 2021, https://socialsciences.uchicago.edu/news/mihaly-mike-csikszentmihalyi-pioneering-psychologist-passes-away-87
2. Mihaly Csikszentmihalyi and Izabela Lebuda, "A window into the bright side of psychology: Interview with Mihaly

Csikszentmihalyi." *Europe's Journal of Psychology,* 13 (2017), 810-821.
3. The Edge.org "Flow: Positive Human Behavior. A Conversation with Mihaly Csikszentmihalyi," August 2004, https://www.edge.org/remembering-mihaly-csikszentmihalyi#intro
4. Csikszentmihalyi and Lebuda, "A window into the bright side of psychology: Interview with Mihaly Csikszentmihalyi."
5. Mihaly Csikszentmihalyi and Reed Larson, "Validity and reliability of the Experience Sampling Method." *The Journal of Nervous and Mental Disease*, 175, no. 9 (1987): 526-36.
6. Ed Diener et al., "An incomplete list of eminent psychologists of the modern era," *Archives of Scientific Psychology,* 2, no.1 (2014): 20-32, http://dx.doi.org/10.1037/arc0000006
7. Martin Seligman and Mihaly Csikszentmihalyi, "Positive psychology: An introduction." *American Psychologist*, 55, no. 1 (2000): 5-14, https://psycnet.apa.org/doi/10.1037/0003-066X.55.1.5
8. Fausto Massimini and Massimo Carli, "The systematic assessment of flow in daily experience." In Csikszentmihalyi, M. and Csikszentmihalyi, I. *Optimal Experience: Psychological studies of flow in consciousness.* (New York: Cambridge University Press, 1988), 266-287.
9. Fausto Massimini, Mihaly Csikszentmihalyi, and Antonella Delle Fave, "Flow and biocultural evolution." In Csikszentmihalyi, M. and Csikszentmihalyi, I. *Optimal Experience: Psychological studies of flow in consciousness.* (New York: Cambridge University Press, 1988), 60-81.
10. Assessing flow: State of the art and challenges for the future." In W. Ruch et al. (Eds.) *Handbook of Positive Psychological Assessment*, (Boston: Hogrefe, 2023), 175-206.
11. https://www.theflowchannel.com/

12. Steimer, "Mihaly "Mike" Csikszentmihalyi, pioneering psychologist, passes away at 87."
13. Steimer, "Mihaly "Mike" Csikszentmihalyi, pioneering psychologist, passes away at 87."

Chapter 3

1. Mihaly Csikszentmihalyi, *Finding Flow: The psychology of engagement with everyday life*. (New York: Basic Books, 1997), 30.
2. Mihaly Csikszentmihalyi and Jeanne Nakamura, "Effortless attention in everyday life: A systematic phenomenology." In B. Bruya (Ed.), *Effortless attention: A new perspective in the cognitive science of attention and action*. (Cambridge, MA: The MIT Press, 2010), 179-190.
3. Csikszentmihalyi and Nakamura, "Effortless attention in everyday life," 182.
4. Roger Ebert, *Awake in the dark: The best of Roger Ebert*. (University of Chicago Press, 2010), 439.
5. Benjamin Hardy, "23 Michael Jordan quotes that will immediately boost your confidence." April, 2016, https://www.inc-aus.com/benjamin-p-hardy/23-michael-jordan-quotes-that-will-immediately-boost-your-confidence.html.
6. April Davila, "16 quotes about getting in the flow," *https://www.inspiringquotes.com/16-quotes-about-getting-in-the-flow/Y0C6PC6-xQAH_jMc*
7. Mihaly Csikszentmihalyi, *Flow: the psychology of optimal experience*. (New York: Harper and Row, 1990), 67.
8. Csikszentmihalyi, *Flow: the psychology of optimal experience*, 2.
9. Csikszentmihalyi, *Flow: the psychology of optimal experience*, 46.

10. James Maddux, "Health, habit, and happiness." *Journal of Sport and Exercise Psychology*, 19 (1997): 344.
11. Susan Jackson, Robert Eklund, and Andrew Martin, *The FLOW Manual.* Mind Garden Inc., https://www.mindgarden.com/100-flow-scales; Susan Jackson and Herbert Marsh, Development and validation of a scale to measure optimal experience: The Flow State Scale. *Journal of Sport and Exercise Psychology*, 18, no.1 (1996): 17-35; Susan Jackson and Robert Eklund, Assessing flow in physical activity: The Flow State Scale-2 and Dispositional Flow Scale-2. *Journal of Sport and Exercise Psychology*, 24, no.2 (2002): 133-150.
12. Susan Jackson, Stephen Ford, Jay Kimiecik, and Herbert Marsh, "Psychological correlates of flow in sport. *Journal of Sport and Exercise Psychology*, 20, no. 4, (1998): 358-378, https://doi.org/10.1123/jsep.20.4.358
13. Susan A. Jackson, "Athletes in flow: A qualitative investigation of flow states in elite figure skaters," *Journal of Applied Sport Psychology*, 4, no.2 (1992): 161-180, https://doi.org/10.1080/10413209208406459

Chapter 4

1. Mihaly Csikszentmihalyi, *Flow: the psychology of optimal experience.* (New York: Harper and Row, 1990), 52.
2. Susan Jackson and Mihaly Csikszentmihalyi, *Flow in Sports: The keys to optimal experiences and performances.* (Champaign, IL: Human Kinetics, 1997), 6.
3. Figure 1 adapted with permission from S.A. Jackson and M. Csikszentmihalyi, *Flow in Sports: The keys to optimal experiences and performances*, (Champaign, IL: Human Kinetics, 1999), 37; and Csikszentmihalyi, M. and Csikszentmihalyi, I. Introduction to part IV. In *Optimal*

Experience: Psychological studies of flow in consciousness. (New York: Cambridge University Press, 1988), 261.
4. Mihaly Csikszentmihalyi, *Finding Flow: The psychology of engagement with everyday life.* (New York: Basic Books, 1997), 32.
5. Figure 2 adapted with permission from Massimini, F., and Carli, M. The systematic assessment of flow in daily experience. In Csikszentmihalyi, M. and Csikszentmihalyi, I. *Optimal experience: Psychological studies of flow in consciousness* (New York: Cambridge University Press, 1988), 270.
6. Benjamin Hardy, "23 Michael Jordan quotes that will immediately boost your confidence." April, 2016, https://www.inc-aus.com/benjamin-p-hardy/23-michael-jordan-quotes-that-will-immediately-boost-your-confidence.html
7. David Bowie interview quote, *https://www.goalcast.com/david-bowie-explains-why-you-should-go-a-little-further-video/*
8. Elizabeth Chai Vasarhelyi and Jimmy Chin (Directors), *Free Solo*. National Geographic Documentary Films, 2018, https://films.nationalgeographic.com/free-solo
9. Richard Ladkani (Director), *Artic Ascent*. National Geographic Documentary Films and Disney+, 2024, https://www.disneyplus.com/en-gb/series/arctic-ascent-with-alex-honnold/49fWWUwfwknH

Chapter 5

1. Psychological Flexibility definition from the Association of Contextual Science, the professional organization of ACT, https://contextualscience.org/the_six_core_processes_of_act
2. Steve Hayes, "Psychological flexibility: How love turns pain into purpose," TED-X talk, February 23, 2016, https://youtu.be/o79_gmO5ppg?si=au0W4kJwW0p_Zr91

3. Akshay Nananvati, https://fearvana.com/
4. Akshay Nananvati, "Find your edges, engage your fear—A radical approach to wisdom." *Finding Mastery* podcast, February 28, 2024, https://findingmastery.com/podcasts/akshay-nanavati-2/

Chapter 6

1. Mihaly Csikszentmihalyi, *Finding flow: The psychology of engagement with everyday life*. (New York: Basic Books, 1997), 128.
2. Carol Dweck, "What having a 'growth mindset' actually means," *Harvard Business Review,* January 13, 2016, *https://hbr.org/2016/01/what-having-a-growth-mindset-actually-means*
3. Carol Dweck, *Mindset: The new psychology of success*. (New York: Random House, 2016), 11.
4. Dweck, "What having a 'growth mindset' actually means," *https://hbr.org/2016/01/what-having-a-growth-mindset-actually-means*
5. Dweck, *Mindset: The new psychology of success*, 20.
6. Dweck, *Mindset: The new psychology of success*, 202
7. John Nicholls, "Achievement motivation: Conceptions of ability, subjective experience, task choice, and performance," *Psychological Review*, 91, no. 3 (1984): 328-346.

Chapter 7

1. Sutra 2-29, *Patanjali's meditation yoga*. Translation and commentary by Vyn Bailey. (Sydney: Simon and Schuster, 1997); BKS Iyengar, *Light on the yoga sutras of Patanjali*. (London: Thorsens, 2002).
2. Sutra 1-2, *Patanjali's meditation yoga*. Translation and commentary by Vyn Bailey.

3. Jon Kabat-Zinn, *Wherever you go, there you are.* (Boston: Little Brown, 1994), 34.
4. Kirk Brown and Richard Ryan, Perils and promise in defining and measuring mindfulness: Observations from experience. *Clinical Psychology: Science and Practice,* 11, no. 3 (2004): 245, https://doi.org/10.1093/clipsy.bph078
5. Kate Pickert, "The Mindful Revolution: The science of finding focus in a stressed out, multitasking culture." *Time,* February 3, 2004.
6. Jon Kabat-Zinn, "What is mindfulness?, https://www.youtube.com/watch?v=HmEo6RI4Wvs
7. Matthew Killingsworth and Daniel Gilbert, "A wandering mind is an unhappy mind." *Science,* 330, no.6006 (2010): 330.
8. Richard Ladkani (Director), *Artic Ascent.* National Geographic Documentary Films and Disney+, 2024, https://www.disneyplus.com/en-gb/series/arctic-ascent-with-alex-honnold/49fWWUwfwknH
9. Ying Hwa Kee and C.K. John Wang, C. (2008). "Relationships between mindfulness, flow dispositions and mental skills adoption: A cluster analytic approach." *Psychology of Sport and Exercise,* 9, no. 4 (2008): 393–411. https://doi.org/10.1016/j.psychsport.2007.07.001
10. Bryan Moore, Propensity for experiencing flow: The roles of cognitive flexibility and mindfulness." *The Humanistic Psychologist,* 41, no. 4 (2013): 41. https://doi.org/10.1080/08873267.2013.820954
11. Stuart Cathcart, Matt McGregor, and Emma Groundwater, "Mindfulness and flow in elite athletes." *Journal of Clinical Sport Psychology,* 8, no.2 (2014): 119-141, https://doi.org/10.1123/jcsp.2014-0018

12. Jeremy Marty-Dugas, Alyssa Smith, and Daniel Smilek, "Focus on your breath: Can mindfulness facilitate the experience of flow?" *Psychology of Consciousness: Theory, Research, and Practice*, 10, no. 3 (2023): 254-280, https://doi.org/10.1037/cns0000251
13. Ka Lo et al., "Examining the feasibility of a mindfulness flow program for Hong Kong archers." *Journal of Clinical Sport Psychology*, published online January 24, 2024: 1-16, https://doi.org/10.1123/jcsp.2023-0029
14. Yi-Yuan Tang et al., "The neuroscience of mindfulness meditation." *Nature Reviews Neurosciences*, 16 (2015): 220.
15. David Rosen et al., "Creative flow as optimized processing: evidence from brain oscillations during jazz improvisations by expert and non-expert musicians." *Neuropsychologia*, 196 (2024): 1-11, https://doi.org/10.1016/j.neuropsychologia.2024.108824
16. Susan Jackson, Robert Eklund, and Andrew Martin, *The FLOW Manual*. Mind Garden Inc., https://www.mindgarden.com/100-flow-scales

Chapter 8

1. James Nestor, *Breath: The new science of a lost art*. (New York: Riverhead/Random House, 2020), Epilogue: A last gasp.
2. Edmund Jacobsen, *Progressive relaxation*. (Chicago: University of Chicago Press, 1929).
3. Herbert Benson and Miriam Klipper, *The relaxation response*. (New York: William Morrow, 1975).
4. Richard Miller, Yoga nidra: *The iRest meditative practice for deep relaxation and healing*. (New York: St Martin's, 2022); see also www.irest.org
5. Sacred Earth, https://www.sacredearthmusic.com/about

6. Susan Jackson, "Stillness and flow." *Australian Yoga Life*, Mar-Jun, 2010.

Chapter 9

1. Phil Jackson and Hugh Delehanty, *Sacred Hoops*. (New York: Hyperion, 1995), 5.
2. Jackson and Delehanty, *Sacred Hoops*, 91.
3. Jackson and Delehanty, *Sacred Hoops*, 174.
4. Jackson and Delehanty, *Sacred Hoops*, 203.
5. George Mumford, *Unlocked: Embrace your greatness, find the flow, discover success.* (New York: Harper One, 2023), 155.
6. Kobe Bryant, Developing a growth mindset. *Sport Science PS*, https://youtu.be/BzmjGk1ICpc
7. April Davila, "16 quotes about getting in the flow," *https://www.inspiringquotes.com/16-quotes-about-getting-in-the-flow/Y0C6PC6-xQAH_jMc*
8. George Mumford, *Unlocked: Embrace your greatness, find the flow, discover success*, 147.
9. Mumford, *Unlocked: Embrace your greatness, find the flow, discover success*, 140.
10. Mumford, *Unlocked: Embrace your greatness, find the flow, discover success*, 151.

Chapter 10

1. Heather Osgood, "5 reasons why podcast advertising has thrived through the pandemic," March 22, 2022, https://www.forbes.com/sites/forbesagencycouncil/2022/03/10/5-reasons-why-podcast-advertising-has-thrived-through-the-pandemic/
2. Oliver Burkeman, "Time, productivity, and purpose: insights from Four Thousand Weeks, interviewed by Peter Attia on

The Drive podcast, #265, August 7, 2023, https://peterattiamd.com/oliverburkeman/

3. Mark Messier, "Leadership, personal growth, and performing under pressure," interviewed by Peter Attia on *The Drive podcast*, #82, December 2, 2019, https://peterattiamd.com/markmessier/

4. Nastia Liukin, "Finish What You Start." *Finding Mastery* podcast, April 24, 2024, https://findingmastery.com/podcasts/nastia-liukin/

5. Jason Hehir (Director), *The Last Dance*, ESPN Films and Netflix, 2020, https://www.netflix.com/au/title/80203144

6. Leslie Tejada, "Remembering ideas," The *Painter's Keys*, March 28, 2008, https://painterskeys.com/thought-walk/

7. Roger Ebert, *Life Itself* (New York: Grand Central Publishing, 2011), https://www.goodreads.com/quotes/881623-when-i-write-i-fall-into-the-zone-many-writers

8. Taylor Schilling, "Face time," *New York Times*, April 20, 2012, https://archive.nytimes.com/tmagazine.blogs.nytimes.com/2012/04/20/face-time-taylor-schilling/index.html

9. Willem Dafoe, interviewed in the *Brisbane News*, October 5-11, 2011.

10. Susan Hornik, "Willem Dafoe On Why He Practices Yoga, the Difficulty of Acting, and Hollywood Stardom," *Yoga Journal*, January 20, 2024, https://www.yogajournal.com/lifestyle/willem-dafoe-yoga/?scope=anon

11. Mihaly Csikszentmihalyi, in Optimal *Experience: Psychological studies of flow in consciousness.* (New York: Cambridge University Press, 1988), 374.

12. Johann Hari, *Stolen focus: Why You Can't Pay Attention.* (London: Bloomsbury, 2022), 58.

13. Mihaly Csikszentmihalyi, *Flow: the psychology of optimal experience*. (New York: Harper and Row, 1990), 41.
14. Csikszentmihalyi, *Flow: the psychology of optimal experience*, 42.
15. Lai-Bao Zhuo et al., "Working life job strain status and cognitive aging in Europe: A 12-year follow-up study." *Journal of Affective Disorders*, 295 (2021): 1177-1183, https://doi.org/10.1016/j.jad.2021.08.114

Chapter 11

1. Mihaly Csikszentmihalyi, "Toward a psychology of optimal experience." In L. Wheeler (Ed.), *Review of Personality and Social Psychology*, (Sage: Beverly Hills, 1982), 13.
2. Susan Jackson and Mihaly Csikszentmihalyi, *Flow in Sports: The keys to optimal experiences and performances*. (Champaign, IL: Human Kinetics, 1997), 142.
3. Richard Logan, "Flow in solitary ordeals." In Csikszentmihalyi, M. and Csikszentmihalyi, I. *Optimal Experience: Psychological studies of flow in consciousness*. (New York: Cambridge University Press, 1988), 172-180.
4. Mihaly Csikszentmihalyi, *Flow: the psychology of optimal experience*. (New York: Harper and Row, 1990), 92.
5. Viktor Frankl, *Man's search for meaning*. (New York: Washington Square Press, 1959), 88.
6. Vincent Deary, *How we break* (2024). Ch 4.2 https://www.audible.com.au/pd/How-We-Break-Audiobook/B0CM41GNKW?action_code=ASSGB149080119000H&share_location=pdp

Acknowledgments

Writing this book has been a long-term goal and one that only by slowing down the pace of my life has led to it coming to fruition. Writing *Experiencing Flow* was never a chore. It became the activity in my day that I most looked forward to. Having a clear purpose and continuously setting present-moment goals throughout the journey resulted in the writing being an enjoyable experience. It is Mihaly Csikszentmihalyi, "Mike," who helped me to find my purpose and to develop clear goals in writing this book. While he was not alive during its writing, my encounters with Mike from when I embarked on graduate studies in the late 1980s until the last time I connected with him in 2020 made it clear to me that flow was an important experience to share. And that it was Mike's conceptualization of flow that was important to uphold. I am forever grateful to Mike for teaching me about flow and for demonstrating how to live a flow-filled life.

I've included in this book the voices of several people who have either manifested flow in their lives and/or advanced flow knowledge through their research and applied work. To Antonella Delle Fave, I thank you for generously sharing your perspective from having worked many years with Mike in advancing flow research. I will always remember your obvious joie de vie that I personally experienced when sharing an Italian meal with you and Mike in Chicago in 1997. Gary and Deanne Gute were the reason I was able to connect online with Mike the year before his death in 2021, and I became intrigued with their work running The Flow Channel. They have each shared valuable insights about Mike through their many years of collaboration and friendship with him, and it has been an enrichment to my life to have found new friends in flow.

Hazel Findlay provides an authentic flow-enriched voice throughout sections of this book, and I thank you, Hazel, for sharing your learnings and perceptions of flow with me and with the readers of this book.

George Mumford, many thanks for your wisdom and positive outlook on life and human experience. And to Kelly Wilson, thank you for being the epitome of an ACT warrior.

My own research in flow would not have been possible without the invaluable insights of the most erudite fellow graduate student I have had the good fortune to work with since the time we met as doctoral students in the early 1990s. Bob Eklund has been a sounding board about all things flow since this time, and the quality of my research and thinking has been positively impacted by his insights. My master's thesis advisor, Glyn Roberts, was open to my idea of interviewing athletes about flow once I stumbled across Mike's first book, *Beyond Boredom and Anxiety*. Glyn taught me to think critically and to aim high with my research endeavors, for which I am grateful. My doctoral advisor, Dan Gould, always encouraged me to pursue my research interests, and I am indebted to his ground-breaking endeavors in qualitative research in sport psychology for helping me to experience the richness of data through interviewing athletes.

Fellow graduate students at the University of Illinois, and later the University of North Carolina-Greensboro, challenged my thinking while simultaneously helping me not to take life too seriously and to enjoy my time living in North America. As did the local triathlon friends I made in Greensboro.

Once I returned home to Australia, I re-connected with my undergraduate honors thesis advisor, Herbert Marsh, who agreed to help me with my research goal of developing and validating a self-report measure to assess flow. Later, Andrew Martin, who had been one of Herb's doctoral students, helped me continue this journey in flow scale development and validation. Bob Eklund contributed significantly at this time to the flow scales, and Bob continues to be my right-hand man for all things flow over 20 years later.

John Hendry helped to re-ignite my motivation to continue to work in the area of flow in Australia when he invited me to first contribute to the Positive Education program at Geelong Grammar School in 2009. John's passion for flow reminded me of why I was studying it, and he has been a wise elder at different times in my journey. Cameron Norsworthy's infectious enthusiasm for flow has contributed to my being involved in work with flow down different avenues and with a wonderful group of flow-seeking individuals through The Flow Centre. Martijn Leonard and Jan van Loon from the Netherlands have shared with me their experiences with and enthusiasm for flow, particularly in the realm of football.

To all the athletes who generously gave their time to my research endeavors and shared their insights and experiences with flow, thank you for enriching my understanding. To the many clients who have been brave in sharing with me their vulnerability and dreams, your resonating with the flow model encouraged me to write this book, to share the flow experience with a larger audience. It has been a joy to work with motivated and intelligent clients facing their unique challenges. Working with you has taught me what was so famously said by Winnie-the-Pooh, "You are braver than you believe."

Thank you to the people who have helped bring this book to publication. Deanne Gute, thank you for your invaluable editing feedback. Your thought-provoking questions helped me to think about ways to improve my writing. To everyone at Authors on Mission, thank you for helping to move this book from a manuscript into published form. And to Patrick Self, thank you for your creative visuals with the flow graphics used in this book (as well as for the author head shot). Thanks also, Pat, for your ongoing encouragement and for creating the www.drsuejackson.com and www.bodyandmindflow.com.au websites to support my work, and for your always insightful feedback.

To the two most important people in my life, my sons Jack and Sean, thank you for your loyalty, your kind hearts, and for always giving me a reason to love. Watching you reach high, follow your dreams, and be the best you can be is a constant source of inspiration to me.

www.ingramcontent.com/pod-product-compliance
Lightning Source LLC
Chambersburg PA
CBHW061808070526
44586CB00024B/2756